The Educator's Guide to Producing New Media and Open Educational Resources

Digital video, audio, and text have never been more popular, and educators need to know how to make new media work in all types of learning environments. *The Educator's Guide to Producing New Media and Open Educational Resources* provides practical advice on how to produce and use open access resources to support student learning. This realistic "how-to" guide is written for education professionals in any discipline seeking to transform their instruction with technology.

Tim D. Green, PhD, is Professor of Educational Technology and former Director of Distance Education at California State University, Fullerton, USA. He co-produces an award-winning podcast with Dr Brown.

Abbie H. Brown, PhD, is Professor of Instructional Technology at East Carolina University, USA. He is an award-winning educator and instructional media designer.

The Educator's Guide to Producing New Media and Open Educational Resources

Tim D. Green and Abbie H. Brown

Routledge
Taylor & Francis Group

NEW YORK AND LONDON

First published 2018
by Routledge
711 Third Avenue, New York, NY 10017

and by Routledge
2 Park Square, Milton Park, Abingdon, Oxon, OX14 4RN

*Routledge is an imprint of the Taylor & Francis Group,
an informa business*

Library of Congress Cataloging-in-Publication Data
A catalog record has been requested

ISBN: 978-1-138-93957-8 (hbk)
ISBN: 978-1-138-93958-5 (pbk)
ISBN: 978-1-315-67486-5 (ebk)

Typeset in Sabon
by codeMantra

For Paul
For Jo, Big Ben, and Bob

Contents

Acknowledgments

We would like to express our appreciation to everyone at Routledge who has had a hand in making this book possible—specifically Daniel Schwartz for his assistance. Finally, we would like to give special thanks to Alex Masulis for listening to our ideas and bringing us opportunities.

New Media and Open Educational Resources Defined

Teachers have been creating educational media for a very, very long time! Beginning with the earliest textbooks written by teachers and designed to help their students better understand course content, and evolving as media production tools became easier to access and use, educators have been producing, reusing, and sharing media for as long as classrooms have existed. In the classroom, traditional production media and tools include bulletin boards, craft paper, butcher paper, felt, magic markers, mimeograph machines, copiers, and computers with printers. Today, there are new media options and open educational resources (OERs) that allow anyone with a networked computer to create and share sophisticated instructional presentations that range from well-designed handouts to elaborate video productions. It is an exciting time to be a teacher, and we consider ourselves fortunate to have an opportunity to share our knowledge of new media and OERs with you.

We have been teaching since the 1980s, and we have been producing digital media to share with our students and colleagues for almost as long. For us, it started with paper banners, signs and cards created with *Print Shop*, and brief interactive multimedia programs produced with *HyperCard* and accessed by students using Macintosh computers with 9" black and white screens. Our successes with digital instructional media led us from our classrooms in Oregon and New Jersey to Indiana University where we met and earned our PhDs in instructional systems technology, to our current positions as professors at California State University, Fullerton (Tim) and East Carolina University (Abbie). Today, we regularly produce, and make available free-of-charge, instructional videos, syllabi, graphics, podcasts, and curated media. We have received a great deal of recognition for our instructional media and are deeply gratified that our colleagues and students find them useful.

For over a quarter of a century, we have been creating and sharing digital resources for teaching and learning, and we are not alone in our efforts. Educators around the world are using new media to produce and share instructional activities we could only once dream of. The purpose of this book is to get you started adding OERs to your instructional practice, creating them using new media, and sharing them with others. Defining the terms "new media" and "open educational resource" is a good place to begin.

New Media Defined

New media is a "catchall term used to define all that is related to the Internet and the interplay between technology, images and sound" (Socha & Eber-Schmid, 2014). It is an all-encompassing phrase for just about any digitally produced piece that combines images, sound, and/or interactivity.

It may help to think of new media as being different from "traditional" media. Traditional media is pretty much everything analog: printed pages, video created and presented using tape, audio on tape or phonograph disk, live theater, television or radio broadcast through the air, and film. If it is media produced and presented without the use of computing tools, it is most likely traditional media. New media is the digital production and presentation of moving images, sound, text, and interactivity. New media is most often networked media as well; it is distributed by placing it in publicly accessible locations on the internet and is most often sharable in that it allows individuals to create links that lead to the media via alternate networks such as Twitter, Reddit, or Facebook.

Open Educational Resources Defined

The higher education information technology organization EDUCAUSE defines OERs as anything that can be used for teaching, learning, or research at little or no cost (EDUCAUSE, 2010). The William and Flora Hewlett Foundation defines OERs as "...teaching, learning, and research resources that reside in the public domain or have been released under an intellectual property license that permits their free use and re-purposing by others... Open educational resources include full courses, course materials, modules, textbooks, streaming videos, tests, software, and any other tools, materials, or techniques used to support access to knowledge" (William and Flora Hewlett Foundation, 2013, p. 16).

Open educational resources or OERs generally refer to digital resources used in online or hybrid learning environments. Digital video, audio, animation, interactive tools, illustrations, infographics, and slide-show presentations are all possible OER formats. Anything one produces digitally and shares at little or no cost with teachers and students can be considered an OER.

If it serves as a teaching tool, is readily available via laptop, desktop, tablet, or smartphone, and is no cost (or low cost) to use, it is an open educational resource or OER produced with new media. Because the terms as we define them encompass a great many varieties of teaching material, the quality of these materials ranges from professionally produced using the state-of-the-art production tools or *"really great"* to amateur productions using inexpensive resources or *"a good start."* The most important measure of any OER, though, is its usefulness as a teaching tool.

Making Use of Open Educational Resources

Educators everywhere can and do make use of OERs. Elementary and secondary teachers in public and private schools, college and university faculty in post-secondary settings, and corporate and government trainers and instructors all regularly employ OERs. University faculty use images, videos, tutorials, homework exercises, eBooks, infographics, audio podcasts, games and simulations, tests and quizzes, and slideshow presentations they find freely available on the internet (Allen & Seaman, 2014). Elementary, middle, and high school teachers are making similar use of OERs (see edutopia.org for a variety of examples), as are corporate trainers and instructional designers (Elkeles, Phillips, & Phillips, 2015).

There is an established tradition of sharing instructional materials among educators. Long before the internet and digital media production, teachers and trainers shared instructional materials with colleagues. Networked new media makes it particularly easy to distribute similar materials, and the low- or no-cost aspects of OERs make them an attractive addition to the textbooks, worksheets, audio-visual media, and software available for purchase.

Video

Instructional videos available via web-based sources such as YouTube, TeacherTube, and Vimeo are used for instruction by embedding the video within a webpage or providing a link to the video. Khan Academy (www.khanacademy.org) is a popular example of a large collection of instructional videos freely available and easily incorporated into online and classroom settings (Figure 1.1).

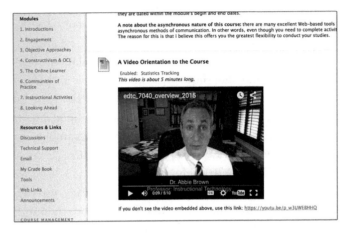

Figure 1.1 An example of a video placed within a course that uses the blackboard learning management system. The video is actually housed on YouTube and is separate from the course itself. It can be reused in other courses and shared using media other than blackboard

Audio

Instructional audios are available in a variety of formats, one of the most popular being podcasts (digital audio available via the internet) through sources such as iTunes and Stitcher. Traditional media networks such as National Public Radio (NPR) also produce and make podcasts freely available (Figure 1.2).

Lesson Plans, Textbook Alternatives, and Curriculum Sharing Sites

There are an almost overwhelming number of sites that provide lesson plans, textbook alternatives, and curricula

Trends &Issues

Instructional Design/Technology

Figure 1.2 Cover art of a podcast. We produce and distribute episodes of the award-winning podcast series, *Trends & Issues in Instructional Design, Educational Technology, and Learning Sciences,* (trendsandissues.com) using our personal computers and software readily available on the internet

Source: Abbie Brown, PhD.

for teachers at every grade level. Edutopia (edutopia.org) is a good place to start looking into the more respected and popular of these. For an example, see the article "Open Educational Resources (OER): Resource Roundup on the Edutopia website" (Edutopia, 2014).

One of the oldest and most respected OER repositories is MERLOT (Multimedia Educational Resource for Learning and Online Teaching: www.merlot.org). The OERs in the MERLOT repository are peer-reviewed, and members of the MERLOT group may create and share their own materials using the MERLOT Content Builder Tool.

The United Nations Educational, Scientific and Cultural Organization (UNESCO) supports the use of OERs worldwide. You can find more about UNESCO's OER initiatives on their website (unesco.org) in the Communication and Information → Themes section (UNESCO, 2015). Another excellent resource for OERs is the OER Commons (www.oercommons.org). The site contains a large number of OER materials and is searchable by subject, grade level (from preschool to adult education), and standards (e.g., Common Core).

Exploring Open Educational Resources

In the following chapters, you will learn how to produce your own OERs. Before you get started, it is a good idea to explore the OERs produced by others that are freely available. You will find things you can use as-is, and you will find inspiration for what you might create on your own. Table 1.1 provides a list of some of the most established and respected OER repositories used for a variety of grade levels.

Exploring the currently available OERs would provide you with ideas for using them in your own instruction

Table 1.1 A list of some of the most established and respected OER repositories available on the internet

Website Name	Web Address
The Internet Archive	archive.org
The Khan Academy	www.khanacademy.org
MERLOT (Multimedia Educational Resource for Learning and Online Teaching)	www.merlot.org
MIT Open Courseware (Massachusetts Institute of Technology)	ocw.mit.edu
OER Commons	www.oercommons.org
Open Ed	www.opened.com
The Open Education Consortium	www.oeconsortium.org
TeacherTube	www.teachertube.com

and inspire you to create OERs of your own. In our experience, creating OERs with new media is an exciting and rewarding activity. As you master new media and gain experience producing OERs, you may find, as we have, new worlds of professional practice that improve and energize you as an educator.

Summary

New Media is a term used to describe any digitally created media; it is often shared via networked computing (the internet, tablet or smartphone apps, etc.). *Open Educational Resources* or *OERs* are any instructional resources that are produced and/or distributed using new media that are available free or at minimal cost. The quality of currently available OERs ranges from expertly produced media to items created by aspiring amateurs. OERs are used in a wide variety of instructional settings, from elementary schools to universities and business settings. A number of excellent OER repositories currently exist and are worth exploring.

2 Digital Video

Video has been an important instructional asset for more than half a century. Broadcast television has been used to effectively teach everything from basic literacy and numeracy (e.g., *Sesame Street*) to university courses for credit (e.g., *Sunrise Semester*). More recently, digital videos presented on the internet have gained in popularity. Websites such as Lynda.com and Khan Academy are examples of vast collections of digital videos that provide instruction on topics ranging from song writing to electrical engineering.

Distribution and Access

Traditional broadcast video requires complex and expensive production and distribution. Producing a single episode of *Sesame Street* costs over $600,000 and requires a large team of professional educators, artists, and technicians. Digital video production can be equally expensive, but it can also be remarkably inexpensive. A single individual can produce highly effective instructional videos using basic computing tools and distributing them through free, web-based resources. As an example, Salman Khan, the founder of Khan Academy, got started with instructional video creating brief mathematics tutorials and distributing them on YouTube.

Distribution of video has also changed dramatically. Access to video in the 1960s and 1970s was largely limited to receiving television broadcasts or accessing closed-circuit networks, both of which are expensive to operate, and opportunities to share locally made videos were extremely limited. In the 1980s and 1990s, the increase in cable television's popularity allowed for a greater variety of channels received as well as opportunities for local producers to share their work via public access channels. Affordable videocassette recorders (VCRs) meant that individuals and institutions could share video using cassette (usually VHS) tapes. Currently, video can be easily distributed over digital networks. Services such as YouTube, TeacherTube, and Vimeo make it easy for anyone with internet access to share video with anyone on the internet.

Digital video is a complex technology that is based on older, analog video models. Digital video is essentially the presentation of computer-generated images and sound: the visual part is presented using pixels (picture elements) which form the building blocks of all digital graphics, and the sound is generated from digitally encoded audio sampling that is converted back to an analog signal for playback. The three elements of video are image, sound, and time. In traditional analog video, the videotape is divided into four sections: image, sound 1 (typically speech), sound 2 (music and/or background noise), and time-code (an electronic signal that indicates temporal location within the presentation). We work with digital video using these same three elements in a computer-based environment.

Digital Video Basics

There are thousands of technical details to learn if you are interested in understanding everything involved in digital video, but for purposes of producing instructional video to share, there are really only a few basic concepts that you need to know:

Frame: The basic unit of video. All video is comprised of still images; each still image is considered a single frame.

Frame Rate: The number of frames shown at a steady rate. This is typically measured in frame per second or "fps"—most video is recorded at 30 fps. In creating the illusion of movement from still images, 10 fps creates a general sense of motion, and 50 fps creates a sense of smooth motion.

Aspect Ratio: The relative width and height of an image or screen. The traditional aspect ratio for television and computer monitors is 4 × 3. The modern aspect ratio for high-definition video and film is 16 × 9. Smartphones and tablet devices are typically 9 × 16 and can be turned sideways for 16 × 9 presentation or recording. See Figure 2.1.

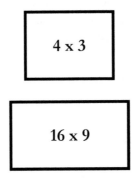

Figure 2.1 Aspect ratios. 4 × 3 is common for computer monitors and older television sets. 16 × 9 is common for newer television sets, smartphones, and tablet devices

Source: Abbie Brown, PhD.

Tracks: Most digital editing software presents the project as a timeline comprised of all the frames in the video. These can be cut, copied, and pasted much like word-processing text. A project can have multiple timelines in layers that work together, and each of these timelines is referred to as a "track." For example, there may be a video track, a track of the narrator's voice, a track for background audio, and a track for the transitions from one video clip to another.

Titles: Text applied like an overlay to recorded video. The most common example of this is in news reporting where written details about what one is viewing are placed at the bottom or in an upper corner of the screen.

Transitions: Images or animations used in video editing to combine scenes. Common transitions are fade-in, fade-out, and dissolve.

Captioning: Providing text for a video's audio content. This is separate from titles in that it is a word-for-word transcription (sometimes with description of other audio cues such as "loud noise" or "applause") and is typically presented as plain text on the bottom portion of the screen.

Compression: The application of algorithmic software to reduce the size of a video file. Compression or codec (compression/decompression) software reduces a video's file size to make it easier to upload and download. Use of compression software usually reduces the video's quality as well.

Encoding: The file formats used for video. Common file formats include .mp4, .avi, and .mov. These files use their own unique compression algorithms to balance video quality and file size.

Streaming: Video that is sent to the user in real time without having to wait for an entire video's file to download. The video is sent as a continuous stream of viewable data to one's device and is typically not saved on the device itself.

How to: Produce Digital Video

The video production process involves scripting and storyboarding, gathering resources, and editing. The entire process can be generally described as developing your vision for the finished video, gathering all the pieces you need, and putting all those pieces together.

The type of editing software you plan to use affects some of the decisions you make in steps that follow. There are a number of software options, and the one you choose depends on your computing hardware and your budget. Since we work on Macintosh platforms and have modest budgets, we prefer Camtasia for Mac by TechSmith. Other popular titles include Windows Movie Maker, iMovie, Final Cut Pro, and Adobe Premiere Pro. As with most media production software, the higher-priced options tend to have a great many more features, but they can also be more difficult to use. If you are new to video production, we recommend starting with something relatively easy to use and inexpensive: Apple's iMovie and Windows Movie Maker are two excellent choices.

Before you begin production, we recommend reading through all of the following steps in order to get a better sense of the entire process.

Scripting and Storyboarding

1. Create a script for the video. The script is a text description of everything that is going to be presented in the video itself. For large and complicated productions, the script is usually a book-length document containing all the dialogue, set descriptions, and transitions from one scene to the next for the entire video. This is especially helpful if a large team is working on the project. The script serves as an important reference point for the crew and cast. For smaller projects, the

script is typically a few pages that serve as the presenter or narrator's talking points. These few pages are important both to keep you on target with the content you wish to present and to help you develop the list of any extra resources (like images or audio files) that you need to complete the video.

2. Create the storyboard. The storyboard is a series of drawn frames showing key moments in the video itself. The frames are the same aspect ratio as the finished product (either 4 × 3 or 16 × 9). This helps you envision the amount of working screen space you have. Next to each frame is a space for production notes that help you remember what you want to show the audience (for example, "presenter steps back to reveal sewing machine previously hidden behind him" or "quick cut to shot of white board with the diagram"—see Figure 2.2). Storyboards are not meant to be works of art; it is perfectly acceptable to draw stick figures and vague shapes. The point is to create a working document that helps you envision how the final product will look.

Gathering Resources

Professionals call the scripting and storyboarding process "pre-production" and the resource-gathering process "production." At this point, you are creating and locating all the media you will need to complete your video. This usually includes finding or creating video clips, graphics, and audio files. At this point, you should also determine the editing software you plan to use and learn which file types you can import into that software.

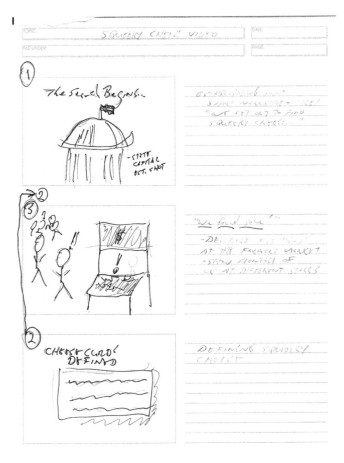

Figure 2.2 Example of a storyboard page. This figure illustrates a hand-drawn storyboard showing three different screens

1. Make a list. Using your script and storyboard, create a list of all the items you need for the video. Once you have your list, it is a matter of gathering each piece listed.

2. Create video clips. You have two options for recording digital video: using a dedicated camera or using a device-embedded camera. Dedicated cameras are the traditional camera-style video recorders; device-embedded cameras are the add-on items that are part of a more complex computing device such as a smartphone, tablet, or laptop. Dedicated cameras tend to be particularly easy to use since they are ergonomically designed specifically to record video, but device-embedded cameras can record very good quality video as well. If you are using a smartphone or tablet device, be sure to turn it on its side to capture video in the best aspect ratio; you want to record 16 x 9, *not* 9 x 16! Once you complete the recording, be sure to save the file in a location that allows you to import it into your editing software and as a file type (encoding format) compatible with your editing software.

3. Find video clips. If you are planning to use video clips from other sources, be sure that they will work within your project's aspect ratio. A video with a 4 x 3 aspect ratio may not work well in a 16 x 9 presentation and vice versa. Make sure that the video clip you wish to use is available from an accessible location and in an encoding format (file type) compatible with your editing software.

4. Create or find audio files. If you are creating video, you can either record sound as part of the video clip, record sound separately to use with the video clip, or find existing sound files to incorporate into your project. As with video clips, be sure that the files you create are saved in an accessible location and as a file type compatible with your editing software.

Editing

Once you have all the resources you need for your video, it is time to blend them together to create the presentation you envisioned with your script and storyboard.

1. Import all of your resources into your editing software (Figure 2.3).

Figure 2.3 This is an image of Techsmith® Camtasia® software. Most video-editing software follows a similar layout with resources located in the upper left corner, a preview panel in the upper right, and the timeline tracks below

Source: TechSmith product screen shot reprinted with permission from TechSmith Corporation.

2. Arrange your resources on tracks in the editor's work area. Creating different tracks for different items such as video, audio, and transitions will make it easier to work with the video. Keep in mind that in most editors, the visual elements are displayed on top of lower tracks: if there are two visual elements that take up the entire screen, the element in the uppermost track will show over visual elements in tracks below it. Each track is part of the larger timeline that is the entire video presentation. Place items where you want them to appear in time when the video plays. For example, place a graphic on its track at the 10-s mark if you want it to display 10 s after the video begins.

3. Test and revise. You can preview the video any time while you are editing. You can pause, rewind, or fast-forward and see the result in the preview window. Preview the video as often as necessary, and make adjustments to the tracks in order to get the exact effect you want (remember to save your work frequently).

4. Save your video as a stand-alone file. This is referred to as "exporting" in many video-editing software options. Once you have the video presentation exactly the way you want it, export the video as a stand-alone file. The file type or encoding you use depends on how you plan to distribute the file. Services such as YouTube accept a wide variety of file types including .mov, mp4, .avi, and wmv. It is best to check which file types are acceptable in advance. You will also have to determine the size of the file by setting the screen size and compression. Larger-screen-size settings require larger file sizes. Compression algorithms or CODECS (this is

short for "compression/decompression") can help reduce file size, but they may also reduce the resolution or clarity of the video. Determining the best size, file type, and compression algorithm is often a matter of trial and error.

How to: Distribute or Broadcast Digital Video

Once you have produced your video, you will need a means to share it with others. If the file is small enough, you could simply send it to individuals as an attachment. However, video files are usually very large, and sending them to individuals does not make the video generally available as an open educational resource. To make your video easily available to others, you will want to make it available via the internet.

Broadcasting your video on the internet requires you to upload the video file to a server space. You can upload your work to either a video-sharing service site such as YouTube or TeacherTube, or a private server space such as a personal website or learning management system. Both approaches are relatively easy to accomplish. However, making use of a video-sharing service will probably provide the largest audience for your work.

Setting Up a Web-Based Video Channel

It is easy to create a video channel. All that is required is to set up a personal account. Services such as YouTube, TeacherTube, and Vimeo allow to you create free accounts.

While YouTube is arguably the most popular service, it is often blocked by K-12 schools because of its broad variety of content. If your videos are designed for a younger audience, you may want to explore a service like TeacherTube that typically has greater access in K-12 settings (Figure 2.4).

Once you have your account set up with a video-sharing service, it is easy to upload video to your account. All services provide a variety of settings that allow you to share the video with the entire world, those with the correct web address for the video, or only with people who have the password you provide. If your video is available to the general public, it is also searchable, meaning that it can be found by anyone using relevant search terms on the internet or within the service itself.

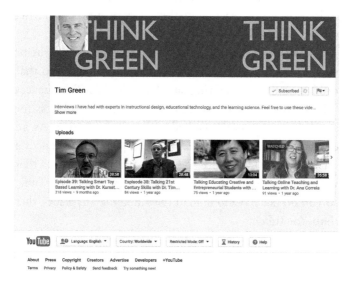

Figure 2.4 Tim maintains an active YouTube channel for his popular *Talking with the Experts* video series

Distributing Video from a Private Website

You can share video from a private website by uploading the video itself to the site's server space and then either providing a link to the file itself or embedding the video in a webpage. Many digital video editors provide an option to save your work as a webpage by creating the video file as well as an html file that has special "embed" code that allows viewers to see the video on the webpage itself. The page the software creates often needs a bit of editing to get it to look exactly the way you want; this can be accomplished by opening the page in a web editor (like Adobe's Dreamweaver) and adjusting the size of the video on the page, adding text above or below, and adding additional links. While distributing video from a private site is possible, it is not as easy as making use of a video-sharing service (Figure 2.5).

Another option to distribute video via a private site or webpage is to use html embed code to display video that resides on a video-sharing site. Sites like YouTube have a "share" option that provides you with a web address for a video as well as the embed code for that video. As an example, this code placed in a webpage's code produces a relatively small viewer that shows a YouTube video on that webpage (it calls the video information from YouTube, so you do not have to upload the video file anyplace other than YouTube):

```
<iframe width="560" height="315" src=
"https://www.youtube.com/embed/LBVyV-
ZI5mA" frameborder="0" allowfullscreen>
</iframe>
```

Abbie Brown at the Society for Information Technology and
Teacher Education (SITE) Conferencein Savannah Goergia

At the SITE Conference
in Savannah, GA 2016

If you can't see the video above, use this link to download the video:

http://www.testbed.com/brown_at_site.mov

Figure 2.5 A .mov file that is both viewable on a webpage
(using html embed code) and downloadable using
the link

You do not have to learn the code construction; you can
easily cut and paste the code provided by the video-sharing
site into the html of any webpage or learning management
system post.

Embedding a YouTube Video in a Webpage

In this example, we use the Weebly web editor.

1. In YouTube, choose the video you want to embed and se-
    lect the Share and Embed options under the video itself
    (see Figure 2.6). Copy the code displayed under Embed.

Figure 2.6 Selecting "Share" and "Embed" on the YouTube site

2. In your web editor, click and drag the "embed code" option to your webpage (see Figure 2.7).

Figure 2.7 The editor with the embed code option dragged to the webpage.

3. Select the HTML option and paste the copied embed code into the HTML window. Once you add the code and exit the editing box, you will see the video "embedded" in the webpage. Think of this as a window that is looking at the YouTube site (see Figure 2.8)

Figure 2.8 Using embed code, the video that resides on YouTube can be viewed on your webpage

Summary

Video is a powerful medium. Video has proven itself to be a useful instructional tool in a wide variety of settings. With its ability to present moving images and sound, it can provide a particularly rich experience for viewers. With our current technology, video can be a bold presentation on a large screen or an intimate sharing moment on a smartphone. Video production tools, which started out as bulky, expensive, and difficult to operate, have become increasingly easy to obtain and use.

Digital video is the direct descendent of traditional analog video. It is easier and less expensive to produce and distribute than its predecessor. Today, many of us carry video production hardware and software around with us in our pockets. Smartphones, phablets, and tablets with video capabilities provide just about everything necessary to create video that looks good even on large monitors and television screens. Sharing these videos with the world is often just a matter of uploading them to an accessible website.

Creating good digital video takes practice, as does gaining confidence and skill in distributing your work. However, the rewards for sharing good video are numerous and varied. Individuals like Salman Khan have seen their digital video work affect students the world over. While our own efforts are not quite as elegant or impactful as the Khan Academy, we are deeply gratified by the positive responses we have received from students and instructors who have used our own modest creations.

Creating and sharing good instructional video require a variety of skills ranging from public speaking to digital editing. While it may not be the easiest medium to master, it may be one of the most effective resources you can provide.

3 Digital Audio

The use of audio for instruction has a long history. For centuries, the spoken word was a principal method used in education. This changed in the mid-15th century with the invention of the printing press and the ability to reach large audiences through the distribution of books and other printed materials. While text remained a dominant medium in education for centuries (and still is currently), the invention in the latter half of the 19th century of the telephone, the phonograph, and the radio brought about an increase in the use of audio for instruction. Since this time, audio has continued to be an important instructional medium as audio production tools have become more readily available and easier to use.

In this chapter, we focus on one type of audio open educational resource (OER)—a podcast. This is by far the longest and most detailed portion of the book, because in our experience, podcasting is currently one of the more challenging OER options to master and, at the same time, one that is often of the greatest interest to educators. We discuss a process and tools that allow you to produce your own podcast. This discussion is based on our experience and knowledge as educational technologists who teach media design and development to educators and as seasoned podcasters who have been producing a podcast show since 2013. The fundamental skills and tools used to produce a podcast that we describe can be used, as well, to create other audio OERs.

Podcasting

The editors of the *New American Oxford Dictionary* declared podcast the word of the year in 2005. As a relatively new medium at that time, podcasting generated a great deal of excitement because of the perceived possibilities for transforming the delivery and listening of audio content. While the excitement for podcasting may have waned after the years immediately following, there is no denying that podcasting has made a recent resurgence in popularity. According to Edison Research (2015), approximately 46 million Americans listen to podcasts monthly in contrast to 22 million in 2006. Of this 46 million, 10% listen to at least one podcast on a weekly basis while the average number of podcasts listened to per week is six.

We see this resurgence being due in part to a number of reasons—the maturation of the medium, the increase in ease of podcast production through the availability of many different development tools, and the number of high-quality podcasts being produced, especially those in the entertainment field (e.g., *Serial*). We have also observed an increase in the number of studies that explore the effectiveness and potential of podcasts as an instructional medium (e.g., Hew, 2009; Heilesen, 2010; Tam, 2012; Collier-Reed, Case, & Scott, 2013; Fernandez, Sallan, & Simo, 2015). Additionally, we have seen the resurgence take place in education at all levels in various instructional contexts. We have noticed an increase in educators' enthusiasm for producing their own podcasts and having their students do the same.

Our foray into podcast production began in 2004 when we began exploring this process, and since late 2013, we have produced our own podcast show. As educational technologists, we view learning how to use new media as being an integral part of our professional development. We explore and learn how new media work in order to facilitate others learning how to effectively design and create their own media. While we know from experience that producing a podcast has become less challenging, there is still a tremendous need for helping educators successfully navigate through the podcast production process. We have written this book for this reason.

Podcasting Defined

The Oxford Dictionary defines podcast as "A digital audio file made available on the internet for downloading to a computer or portable media player, typically available as a series, new installments of which can be received by subscribers automatically" (Oxford Dictionaries, nd). The word podcast can be used as either a noun, referring to the content (e.g., a single podcast episode), or as a verb, referring to the method of delivery. Podcasting has been referenced in popular media including magazines, newspapers, and news-oriented websites since late 2004 (Brown & Green, 2008). The term podcast is a blend of the brand name, "iPod," Apple's famous portable media player originally released in 2001, and the word, "broadcast" (pod + cast).

We find that there can be misconceptions about what is a podcast. A podcast is not simply an audio file that is available on the internet for listening. What makes a podcast a podcast is the process of automatic delivery (through a Really Simple Syndication (RSS) feed; see Chapter 5) of new podcast episode audio files to an individual who has subscribed to that podcast. The new podcast episodes are delivered through software in a format that allows the subscriber to listen to the episodes.

We often compare this process to a traditional paper-based newspaper subscription. As you read the following example, consider the newspaper being the podcast and the daily newspaper issues being the podcast episodes. Abbie enjoys reading *The New York Times*. He could go out every morning to his local newsstand to purchase that day's issue of the paper, but this would be highly inconvenient. He might find that he does not have the time to do this every day. He could forget to do this from time to time. He could go to the newsstand late in the afternoon and find that all copies of that day's issue have been sold. In order to avoid these scenarios, Abbie would subscribe to the newspaper and have it delivered directly to his house. Then, every morning after he has gotten out of bed, he could go out his front door to find that day's issue waiting for him on his front porch.

Podcasting's Development as a Medium

Web radio has been around since the mid-1990s (Ciccarelli, n.d.). Like traditional radio, one could listen to a continuous, synchronous feed of audio content from a provider without the option to play specific programs at one's convenience. The original podcasting process was developed by former MTV veejay and internet entrepreneur Adam Curry, who helped produce *iPodder* software, which facilitated the routing of audio files to digital music players. Curry worked with Dave Winer, the creator of RSS, which forwards internet-based text feeds to subscribers, to create a method of sending audio files through RSS (Brown & Green, 2008).

Podcasting's development in the early 2000s allowed listeners to access audio content asynchronously, allowing the listener to download and play specific episodes or subscribe to a show series. In 2005, the editors of the *New American Oxford Dictionary* declared podcast to be their word of the year—an indication of podcasting's popularity in the first few years of its development. In those early years, however, the process of subscribing to and downloading podcast episodes was challenging (Kang, 2014), and series content was often obscure and of limited interest.

Farhad Manjoo, writing for *The New York Times*, states, "While the medium is more than a decade old, from the moment the very first pods were cast, people have been calling podcasting either the world's next great media revolution, or another failed byway in digital experimentation"

(Manjoo, 2015). In February of 2015, Edison Research reported that an estimated 46 million Americans (17% of the population) over the age of twelve had listened to at least one podcast within the past month (Edison Research, 2015). The growth among podcast listeners has been slow but steady over the past decade (Manjoo, 2015; Edison Research, 2015), with over 30% annual growth in recent years (Parvizi & Silverman, 2015).

While podcasting has always been closely associated with Apple products and services, competing organizations have attempted to embrace and capitalize on podcasting as well. For example, the content site Google Play, which sells media content for Android devices, now supports podcast creators and allows users to download podcasts from the Play site (Bergen, 2015). With the increase in podcasting products on Apple and Android devices, podcasts have become increasingly easier to subscribe to and download. Bluetooth-enabled cars, smartphones, and tablet devices allow listeners to quickly and easily load up and listen to programs, and access to programming is no longer limited to RSS or iTunes (Kang, 2014).

Using Podcasts as an Instructional Tool

While our focus is on the podcast production process and helping you learn how to create your own podcast, we would feel remiss if we did not give some attention to how podcasts and podcast production could be used instructionally. We view podcasting as a creation activity or a consumption activity. As a creation activity, podcasting can be used to teach and reinforce a number of skills. You can teach your

learners—like we are doing with you through this book—
how to design, record, and edit audio and publish a podcast.
They would learn a number of multimedia design and development skills. During this process, your learners could
practice critical-thinking and problem-solving skills. Having your learners work in teams would give them opportunities to work on collaboration skills as well. Additionally, the
content of the podcast can provide learners with the opportunity to demonstrate content knowledge. As a consumption
activity, podcasting can provide your learners with access to
a wide range of content from experts and organizations that
your learners can consume. You can provide your students
content as well through a podcast that you produce.

How to: Producing a Podcast

There are several steps in creating your own OER podcast. The production process includes three major phases:
design, development, and distribution. Within each phase
are multiple steps. We outline each step as we discuss the
three phases. You can create your own podcast by following the steps we have provided.

Designing a Podcast

Before you begin producing and sharing your podcast, you
will need to consider the format and design of your show.
Are you creating a single, stand-alone show or a series
with multiple episodes? What is the time length for the
show or episodes? How often do you plan to release new

shows? What is each show's format? There is a great deal to consider before you press the "record" button.

As an example, here is the current format of our podcast, *Trends & Issues in Instructional Design, Educational Technology, and Learning Sciences*:

- It is a podcast series, with new episodes uploaded every 2 weeks.

- Each episode is approximately 10 min long.

- Each episode begins and ends with the same "bumpers" of narration spoken over music. The opening bumper states the title of the series and the names of the hosts. The closing bumper states the title of the series and the names of the producers.

- After the opening bumper, Tim and Abbie say hello with their standard greeting, "Hi, this is Tim and I'm here with Abbie. Hi, this is Abbie and I'm here with Tim." Tim then explains that we are reviewing the trends we have observed over the past 2 weeks, making reading recommendations based on what we collected in our *Flipboard* magazine over the past 2 weeks, and making predictions about future trends.

- Abbie then states the three or four major trends identified within the past 2 weeks.

- Tim transitions to the recommended readings segment. Abbie provides the titles, authors, sources, and brief commentary.

- Tim transitions to the "crystal ball" segment. Abbie describes what they consider to be the educational technology trends and issues on the horizon.

- Tim concludes by reminding the audience of the team's *Flipboard* magazine, the Trends and Issues website, and that the podcast is available through iTunes and Stitcher. Tim's final statement is the date for the next podcast episode release.

- The podcast episodes are titled primarily by number, with secondary information related to the dates and content the episode covers. Example: "Episode 51 Trends for Weeks of November 9–23 VR Applications, Online Learning, and Apple Products" (Figure 3.1).

Instructional Design/Technology

Figure 3.1 Cover art for Trends and Issues Podcast. This image illustrates the cover art we created that follows the requirements outlined by Apple to submit a podcast to iTunes

Source: Abbie Brown, PhD.

Not only did we design the show's format, but we also designed promotional artwork for the podcast as well. This design conforms to Apple's artwork specifications for iTunes. We recommend that you consider creating artwork that helps to identify and promote your podcast as well.

Before we set the format for our podcast series, we made a number of design decisions:

- Episodes are intended to provide an overview of the most prominent trends and issues in educational technology reported in the media over the past 2 weeks. Before recording an episode, Abbie and Tim review their *Flipboard* magazine, identifying trends derived from the articles collected, selecting those articles that are particularly interesting and important to recommend to their listeners, and discussing what they consider to be upcoming trends to watch.

- The presentation style is conversational. Abbie and Tim speak casually with each other, occasionally making jokes and laughing, in each segment.

- Each episode is deliberately designed to be around 10 min long. Regular episodes vary in length, but rarely by more than a few minutes.

The design and format of our series, *Trends & Issues in Instructional Design, Educational Technology, and Learning Sciences*, was developed from initial conversations between us, mapping out key elements such as the bumpers and the three major segments, based on the content we provide, compatible formats we liked in the podcasts, and shows we follow personally. Even with the general format in place, there was a good deal of trial and error in producing the first ten episodes. We listened to those first podcasts to decide what we did and did not like, and we listened to feedback from listeners who shared their ideas with us. The design and format of the series is pretty well set at this point, but we still regularly discuss and consider changes. As you consider your own show's design, you may want to write down your key design considerations and keep this nearby to serve as a template and a reminder of the structure of your show.

Episodes, Seasons, and Series

The first design consideration is the number of shows you will be producing. Planning to produce a single show is different from planning to produce a series. In a series, each episode should share common elements that make the show a recognizable part of the series as a whole. This is where bumpers can be particularly helpful. Bumpers are the beginning and ending segments of the show (hence their name). The most common example of this for most of us is television theme songs. Most half-hour television comedies, for example, begin and end each of their episodes the same way; look at any episode of *The Simpsons*, and you'll see the opening and closing music and animation is the same. Since the bumpers are meant to be the same for each show, you can produce them in advance and reuse them each time you produce a new episode.

Naming the shows produced is another design consideration. If you are producing a single show, the name should indicate the show's content as completely as possible in a brief phrase. If you are producing a series, the series itself needs a name and each episode gets its own unique name. The unique name of an episode, however, should in some way relate to the other episode names. The television series *Friends*, for example, has a unique name for each episode, but they all begin with the phrase *The One* (*with, in,* or *about*); the final episode of the series is titled *The Last One*. Episode titles can be as elaborate and clever as word play, or they can be as simple as the episode's numeric place in the series (e.g., *Episode 18*).

If you plan to produce a series, you will want to consider whether the series will be organized by seasons or whether it will be ongoing. Seasons indicate a subset of episodes collected together based on the time they are produced; a season might be all episodes produced in a single year, for example. Our *Trends & Issues* podcast, for example, is organized as ongoing with episode numbers but no indication of seasons.

Format

Any show you produce will have a format. The only format we do *not* recommend is one where you begin to record and just ramble on. Before you begin to record your first show, we recommend that you make at least two design decisions: decide how long the show will be, and decide what major segments the show will contain.

The first consideration, show length, depends on the amount of content you intend to share and how you envision the listener interacting with the show. As an example, our *Trends & Issues* podcast episodes are deliberately about 10 min long because we assume that the vast majority of our listeners are busy professionals and students who listen in to get a quick update of the current trends in our field. You may find yourself designing shows for a similar audience, or you might find yourself designing more detailed shows that require a longer run time in order to more fully immerse the audience in the content. If you plan to produce a series, we recommend that each episode be roughly the same length so that listeners know what to expect and what to look forward to (the exceptions are special episodes that may be longer or shorter because of the content).

The major segments of the show should be planned in advance as well. The most obvious segments of any show are the beginning, middle, and end, but that may not provide you with enough of a template for production. Segments are the organization of the show's content; decide upon your segments the same way you would approach presenting a lesson, by determining the activities that make up the lesson. For our *Trends & Issues* podcast, we divide each episode into three major segments: what is trending, recommended readings, and prediction of future trends. This is similar to what we might do if we were presenting a lesson on the same topic. If you plan to produce a series, the segments you decide upon help create a formula for each new episode. This formula helps you determine what to present. Perhaps more importantly, the formula helps your podcast subscribers listen effectively by providing a reliable frame of reference.

Scheduling

If you plan to produce a podcast series, scheduling becomes an important design consideration. There are a wide variety of schedule options, ranging from releasing an episode randomly, whenever one is ready (perhaps one in January, another in March, and another in November), to releasing a daily episode at the same each day (perhaps every morning at 9:00 AM Pacific Standard Time). There is no single best scheduling approach; the scheduling you choose depends on the content and listening experience you wish to provide. For our *Trends & Issues* series, we have chosen to release brief episodes every 2 weeks because we find this to be the best way to keep up with educational technology news reports posted in journals, magazines, blogs, and newspapers. Whatever option you decide upon, we recommend adhering to the schedule you set for yourself because this is a good way to gain a positive reputation and build your listening audience.

Elements to Consider with Design

As you consider the design of your podcast, take into consideration whether you are planning to produce a single episode or a series of episodes. If you are planning a series, consider whether you want to organize the series into a set of seasons or have it run as a single, continuous set of shows. Decide upon the general length of each show or episode in advance. Consider how best to organize your content into segments; develop a template or formula of segments if you're planning a series of episodes. Finally, consider the scheduling for multiple episodes; decide how often you plan to release new shows.

Although most of your design decisions will be based on the content you plan to provide and the audience you wish to reach, you should also consider yourself as both a resource and a limiting factor in what you plan to offer. You can only produce and distribute as much as you have time to create. As an example, it takes us about 4 h to produce a single, 10-min episode of our *Trends & Issues* podcast; we both schedule this effort into our professional routine twice a month and this works well for us. Your own podcast format will have to fit your schedule.

Developing the Podcast

Once you have determined the format and design of your podcast, you are ready to begin production. This is when you can start hearing your work come to life! Producing your podcast involves three general steps—recording, editing, and publishing. Within each of these steps, there are a number of possible production paths. Our goal is to help you create your podcast as quickly as possible; therefore, we are only describing the process we use rather than sharing the many different variations. As you gain experience with creating podcasts, you may find that you end up modifying the process we describe.

The Necessary Tools

Producing a podcast requires certain tools. Most likely, you either own or have easy access to the tools that you need. At the minimum, you will need a computer, a microphone, and audio recording and editing software. We recommend you also have headphones; however, headphones are not absolutely necessary. Versions of these tools range in price and quality; some of them can be quite expensive. We suggest starting out with inexpensive tools and only the ones you absolutely need—experiment with the production process before purchasing additional tools or more expensive tools. Let's explore the specific tools that we use.

MICROPHONES

To produce a clear and robust sounding podcast, a high-quality microphone is crucial. While you could spend hundreds of dollars—or even thousands—on a microphone, we suggest that you start out simple. When we began our podcast, we used the best and most cost-effective option we had available—headsets with microphones attached. We used this option for several episodes with success; it was a great way to start because it allowed us to establish our podcast in a low-cost way. During our first full year, however, we eventually determined that if we were to improve the sound quality of our podcast an upgrade was necessary. We discovered there were a number of different options and issues to consider and, based on recommendations that we read from seasoned podcasters and our own investigation, we chose USB microphones from the company called Blue Microphones (http://bluemic.com). Tim uses the Yeti Blue, and Abbie uses the Snowball. These microphones are relatively inexpensive ($100 or less), easy to set up, simple to use, and capable of recording high-quality audio directly into recording and editing software.

AUDIO RECORDING AND EDITING SOFTWARE

Capturing your audio can be accomplished using a number of different software options. We suggest using software that you have readily available (e.g., GarageBand) and are comfortable using. The specific software we recommend is Audacity (http://audacityteam.org). Audacity is free, cross-platform software that allows you to record and edit your audio. Despite being free, it is sophisticated, and it is well supported by its developers.

While we use Audacity to edit our audio, we have used different software to capture our audio. We started with Call Recorder (http://ecamm.com; $29.95). Because we live in two different locations—California and North Carolina—we conduct our podcast episodes using Skype. We needed a tool that allowed us to easily capture our Skype conversations. Call Recorder is designed specifically to capture Skype conversations by taking both audio feeds and creating a single file. This file can be imported into another software to be edited. We now use QuickTime because we have found that the quality of our audio is higher when using this software (more about this in the Recording the Audio section).

It is important to note that Call Recorder only works on the Apple OS. There are options for recording Skype calls on the Windows operating system, but we have not used them ourselves. We suggest doing an internet search using the phrase "recording Skype on Windows"; this will bring up a listing on Skype's website that lists a number of different tools that work on Windows. Figure 3.2 is a screen grab of the listing of available software at the time we wrote this book.

Program Name	Supported OS	Website Link
Amolto Call Recorder	Windows Vista or newer	Click Here
Callnote Premium Call Recorder	Windows or Mac OS X	Click Here
CallTrunk for Skype	Any	Click Here
eCamm Call Recorder for Skype	Mac OS X	Click Here
Evaer	Windows XP or newer	Click Here
Evoca Call Recorder	Mac OS X	Click Here
G-Recorder	Windows or Mac OS X	Click Here
iRecorder	Windows XP or newer	Click Here
MP3 Skype Recorder	Windows Vista or newer	Click Here
Pamela	Windows XP or newer	Click Here
TalkHelper	Windows Vista or newer	Click Here
Tapur	Windows and Mac OS X	Click Here
Vodburner	Windows and Mac OS X	Click Here
Xsplit	Windows XP or newer	Click Here

Figure 3.2 Listing from Skype's Website of Software for Recording Skype Calls

HEADPHONES

As mentioned, headphones are not necessary. While there are differing opinions by audio recording experts about the use of headphones during the recording process, we suggest using headphones for three reasons. The first is to cut down on feedback or echoes that can occur during the recording process. We found that without headphones, there was a tendency to hear an echo when we were connected using Skype. When we used headphones during recording, this was eliminated. Even if you do not use Skype, your microphone can pick up and record the sound coming from your computer speakers. Wearing headphones can eliminate this. The second reason is that we believe headphones can help cut out extraneous noises we hear while recording, thus giving us a higher level of focus during recording. The final reason is that headphones allow us to more clearly hear the audio during editing. As such, we are better able to make needed adjustments and edits to our final product.

The Development Process

Once you have the necessary tools, you are ready to begin the production process. We have refined our process since starting our podcast in December 2013. We will walk you through the steps we take recording, editing, hosting, and publishing our podcast.

CREATING BUMPERS

One of the first things you will create for your podcast is a set of bumpers—one for the beginning and one for the end of your podcast episodes. As we described earlier in the chapter, bumpers are meant to be the same for each show to help establish a consistent experience for listeners; as such, you will want to produce them in advance and reuse them each time you produce a new episode. Podcast bumpers typically include a mixture of narration and music. They are relatively short—about 10–30 s.

Our bumpers introduce the title of our show and let listeners know who we are and with what institutions we are affiliated. Abbie created our bumpers using GarageBand. He created the narration and used modestly priced music purchased from a royalty-free music site. We chose to purchase music because we could not find free music we liked nor did we have the skill necessary to easily create our own. There are a number of websites that offer royalty-free music. You can search on the internet using the phrase "royalty-free music for podcasts" to find a listing of these sites. Unless you have the skill to create your own, you are most likely going to need to purchase music for your bumpers.

PRE-RECORDING

Earlier in the chapter, we described a number of design decisions you need to consider prior to recording your first show. Are you creating a single, stand-alone show or a series with multiple episodes? What is the time length for the show or episodes? What is each show's format? Once you have these decisions made, you are able to focus on the specific topics and ideas you will discuss during your show. For each episode, we suggest developing an outline of the topics and ideas you will include. You will be much more focused during your recording of the audio if you have an outline. How detailed you make the outline depends on your own preference and the content and the format of the show.

For our podcast, we put together a brief outline of notes for each episode that is based on the show's three segments: trends, recommended readings, and crystal ball trend predictions. On the day we record an episode, we typically spend 30 min discussing and compiling our ideas immediately before recording. We use a collaborative web-based tool (currently Google Docs) where we record the notes. Having the notes keeps us around the 10-min time frame we strive to keep for each episode. Additionally, the notes are the basis for our "show notes" that we include on our blog (see *Step 3 Publishing: Making the Podcast Available to the World*).

RECORDING THE AUDIO

The method used to record the audio for your show is greatly influenced by whether you are producing the show alone or if you have others involved either as co-hosts or as guests. As mentioned, with our podcast we had to determine how to record two audio feeds because we live on opposite sides of North America. We experimented with different tools before determining that connecting with Skype was our best option. Skype allows us to have a live conversation at a distance that can be recorded using audio recording software. We initially used Call Recorder to capture the audio, but we have now switched to QuickTime. While Call Recorder is highly convenient—it records both of our audio feeds and saves them as one audio file—we have switched to QuickTime because we determined that the audio can be recorded at a higher quality when using this tool. The downside to using QuickTime is that we need to record our own audio feeds. As such, we have two audio files rather than one, which increases the amount of work during the production process.

Despite the specific circumstances we have had to work through, the process we use is one that you can follow with slight modifications that fit your specific situation. The following are the steps we take in recording the audio for our show:

1. **Connect via Skype.** We connect via Skype with audio and video. We find that being able to see each other helps with the flow of the show because we can give visual clues to each other. Once connected, we check our volume levels and sound quality, adjusting as necessary before recording.

2. **Discuss Show Content.** We discuss the content for the show and create our outline of the three segments on a shared Google doc. Our introduction and closing comments of our show have stayed relatively the same since the start of the podcast. Earlier in the chapter, we described what we typically say in our introductions and closing comments.

3. **Test Audio.** We record approximately 15–30 s of audio to ensure that we are picking up the audio feeds and the quality is high.

   - When we used Call Recorder, Tim controlled the recording on his computer. Tim would verbally indicate that the record button was about to be clicked. Once the recording started, we practiced the podcast opening. Tim would stop the recording and save the file. Tim would locate the file on his computer to listen to the audio to determine its quality. We adjusted our recording devices (e.g., raising or lowering microphone recording volume) if needed. If not, we moved on to recording the episode.

- Now that we use QuickTime, our process is slightly different. Rather than creating one audio file that Tim records from his computer, we have separate audio files that we each record. When we are ready to test the audio, we both click on the record button on the QuickTime software running on our computers to capture our individual audio. We will practice the introduction, stop the recordings, save the files, and individually test the quality. We make adjustments as necessary.

- As a side note, using a tool like Call Recorder is a good option if you are interviewing a guest who is at another location. This way you are not relying on your guest to record and send you an audio file. If you are in the same location as your co-host or guest, you could use QuickTime or another audio recording software that you are comfortable using.

- It is critically important to test out the audio to make sure your audio levels are acceptable. Do not skip this step. It is difficult to fix audio during the editing process that has been recorded at a loud level because the audio often can be distorted. The microphones we use have a *Gain* control knob that allows us to adjust the recording level. If your microphone does not, you can adjust the recording level directly in the software you are using. With QuickTime on the Apple OS, you will need to adjust your recording level by going to the System Preferences > Sound > Input.

- You should also test out the audio quality by practicing at different distances from your microphone. Typically, the best audio quality will be recorded if you are directly in front of your microphone within a few inches.

- You will want to do your best to cut down on extraneous sounds because these can also be difficult to edit out of the final audio. You will want to turn off your cell phone and other devices. You will want to limit your movements and not bump, tap, or hit where you have your microphone located. Finally, be aware of your breathing, sniffles, and coughs—especially when you are recording with someone else and you are listening rather than talking. We have learned from experience that our microphones are extremely sensitive. Tim did a solid—albeit, unexpected—Darth Vader impersonation during one of our recordings when he had a cold because he was breathing rather loudly and was too close to his microphone. Understandably, we had to record this episode a second time.

- Finding the right recording levels and a suitable location to record will take some experimentation. While we have improved our audio quality over time, we still continue to work on improving it.

4. **Record Podcast Episode.** Once the audio quality check is finished, recording of the episode begins. Tim will verbally indicate that he is going to click the record button on QuickTime. Abbie will verbally indicate the same. Once the recordings have started, Tim will visually count down with his fingers from 3, 2, 1, and then begin the introduction—"Hi. This is Tim, and I am here with Abbie." The podcast recording is underway.

   ● It is important to consider how comfortable you are with the editing process and how much time you have to devote to it. Both will have an impact on how you approach recording. It is nearly impossible not to have to edit—at the minimum, you will need to add your bumpers to your episode audio. We are comfortable with the editing process. We do not worry as much about making mistakes during recording as we did during the first few episodes we recorded. While we do try to limit slipups, they are not a major issue. If one occurs during recording, we will keep recording the audio; we will pause, collect our thoughts, and continue on because we are able to delete these sections out during editing. Additionally, now that we record two audio files since we started using QuickTime, we have added to the amount of time needed to edit because we have two audio files rather than one that needs to be edited.

5. **Gathering the Two Audio Files.** Once the three segments of the episode are complete, Tim stops his recording and Abbie does the same. Each saves his

individual file. Abbie sends his file to Tim for editing. Abbie sends the file to Tim through Skype. The files tend to be large, and we have used other transfer methods such as Google Drive and Dropbox when Skype is unable to handle things.

EDITING THE AUDIO

Now that you have your audio recorded, you will need to edit it to create the finished podcast episode file that you will publish and share with the world. Tim edits our podcast using the following process:

1. **Create a Folder and File Structure.** It is important to consider how you will name and store the files you create as you produce your podcast. While you will only need to create this structure once, we include it as one of the steps because it is an important reminder to properly name your files when saving them. A well-thought-out, consistent structure ensures that you are working with the most current file version and that you only share an episode that is complete. Let's take a look at how we structure our folders and files. It may seem complicated at first glance, but it truly is not. We find that this structure helps us to stay organized, and we believe it will do the same for you.

   - Figure 3.3 shows our folder structure. Each episode has its own folder name based on the episode number (e.g., *038_episode*). The folders you see for each episode are located within a folder we named *trends_podcast_episodes*. In addition to the episode folders, we also have our artwork image file and the bumper audio files located here. We also have a folder named *images_podcast* that includes images we use on our podcast blog (we'll discuss the blog in depth later in the chapter).

- To save time, we have a folder titled *generic_episode* that we duplicate and rename for the current episode we are producing. This folder includes the two folders (shown in Figure 3.3) you will need for each episode.

- Figure 3.3 shows the structure of a podcast episode folder along with the files that make up an episode. This figure shows the contents of a folder named *055_episode* (our 55th podcast episode). There are two folders—*published* and *raw_audio*—within this folder. Within these two folders you can see the audio files for episode 55. The one file (MP3) in the published folder is the final version of episode 55 that was published. The files in the *raw_audio* folder are our working files. The file with the AUP (Audacity audio project) extension is an Audacity audio file. The folder named *055_eps...nds_data* goes along with this file—Audacity automatically creates a folder for each audio project created using Audacity. You do not have to worry about what is in this folder. The remaining two files are the audio files (M4A) that Abbie and Tim recorded and saved during the episode recording using QuickTime.

- We recommend that you are consistent with naming your files. We suggest using all lowercase and avoid using spaces. We use an underscore (_) rather than a space. For our QuickTime files, we use the following convention: *firstname_episode_episode-number* (which translates to *tim_episode_055*). Our final podcast file follows a consistent naming convention as well: *055_episode_trends_podcast*. The only part of the file name that changes from episode to episode is the episode number (Figure 3.4).

Name	^	Date Modified	Size	Kind
▶ 038_episode		May 6, 2015, 7:33 AM	--	Folder
▶ 039_episode		May 6, 2015, 7:33 AM	--	Folder
▶ 040_episode		Jun 2, 2015, 3:14 PM	--	Folder
▶ 041_episode		Jun 19, 2015, 6:32 PM	--	Folder
▶ 042_episode		Jul 14, 2015, 11:55 AM	--	Folder
▶ 043_episode		Jul 27, 2015, 12:49 PM	--	Folder
▶ 044_episode		Aug 17, 2015, 6:35 PM	--	Folder
▶ 045_episode		Aug 30, 2015, 10:40 AM	--	Folder
▶ 046_episode		Sep 17, 2015, 9:10 AM	--	Folder
▶ 047_episode		Sep 28, 2015, 10:31 AM	--	Folder
▶ 048_episode		Oct 15, 2015, 11:54 AM	--	Folder
▶ 049_episode		Oct 26, 2015, 1:33 PM	--	Folder
▶ 050_episode		Jul 27, 2015, 8:57 AM	--	Folder
▶ 051_episode		Jul 27, 2015, 8:57 AM	--	Folder
▶ 052_episode		Dec 7, 2015, 3:10 PM	--	Folder
▶ 053_episode		Dec 23, 2015, 10:56 AM	--	Folder
▶ 054_episode		Today, 2:39 PM	--	Folder
▶ 055_episode		Yesterday, 3:58 PM	--	Folder
▶ generic_episode		Today, 2:38 PM	--	Folder
▶ images_podcast		Apr 20, 2015, 5:57 PM	--	Folder
podcast_co...n_green.jpg		Dec 25, 2013, 1:19 PM	628 KB	JPEG image
trends_issu...er_01b.mp3		Sep 23, 2013, 3:32 PM	242 KB	MP3 audio
trends_issu...er_02b.mp3		Sep 23, 2013, 3:32 PM	242 KB	MP3 audio

Figure 3.3 Folder Structure We Use for Storing Podcast Episode Files

Name	^	Date Modified	Size	Kind
▼ published		Today, 2:38 PM	--	Folder
055_epis...nds.mp3		Today, 2:37 PM	13.1 MB	MP3 audio
▼ raw_audio		Today, 2:38 PM	--	Folder
▶ 055_epis...nds_data		Today, 7:03 AM	--	Folder
055_epis...ends.aup		Today, 7:03 AM	44 KB	Audaci...Project
abbie_ep...._55.m4a		Yesterday, 10:18 AM	29.1 MB	Apple...4 audio
tim_epis...e_55.m4a		Yesterday, 10:10 AM	20.8 MB	Apple...4 audio

Figure 3.4 Typical Files in a Folder for an Episode

2. **Gather Raw Audio.** Once you have your folder structure in place, you need to gather your unedited or "raw" audio and put these files in the correct locations.

   - At this point in the production process of an episode, we have two files in our *raw_audio* folder: a file with Abbie's audio and a file with Tim's audio recorded using QuickTime. These files are M4A files. These are the first two files that Tim edits.

3. **Edit Content.** Editing the audio content requires a number of steps. The process will seem complicated initially. However, once you have gone through this process a few times, it does become easier.

   - In Audacity, Tim opens the two M4A files mentioned in step 2. Figures 3.5 and 3.6 are examples of what these audio files look like when opened in Audacity.

   - Tim listens to each audio file. As he listens to the audio files, he makes edits to the content by deleting "umms" and spots where we slipped up. Deleting portions of an audio file is referred to as *clipping*—you are highlighting a portion of the audio and then deleting it. As you may imagine, this can be a tedious process. You should find that as you gain experience recording episodes, the number of edits decreases because your delivery of the content improves. You should also find that you become more efficient with editing the content. Be patient; effective delivery and editing both take practice.

- After cleaning up the two audio files, Tim begins the process of turning the two files into one. He copies the portion of his audio that is the introduction—"Hi. This is Tim, and I am here with Abbie." He will then insert (i.e., paste) this audio right before the spot in Abbie's file where Abbie says, "Hi. This is Abbie, and I am here with Tim." As a side note, copying and pasting portions of the audio from one audio file to the other audio file in Audacity is similar to copying and pasting text from one word processed document to another. You highlight the portion you want to copy; you copy it; and then paste it in the location on the other file where you want the copied portion to be located. Make sure to include some space (that is, "silent" audio with no talking) between the two portions of the audio. This space will provide a natural transition between the two audio clips.

- At this point, Tim will save Abbie's file as an Audacity Project. We mentioned above that when you save a file in Audacity it creates a project that includes an Audacity audio file (AUP) and a folder with a number of files in the folder (do not worry about what is in the folder). Save the Audacity Project as the name of your podcast episode (e.g., *055_episode_podcast_trends*). This is now your working file. You will still have the two audio files opened that you started with (Figures 3.5 and 3.6). One will just be renamed. Make certain to save the Audacity project in the *raw_audio* folder.

● Tim will continue the process of copying portions of his audio file and paste into Abbie's audio file until the entire episode is put together.
As a side note, Tim will save the Audacity project each time he copies and pastes an audio portion. Figure 3.7 shows what a typical completed
podcast episode file looks like after the two
QuickTime (M4A) files (Figures 3.5 and 3.6) are
converted into one.

● Tim then exports this file (Figure 3.7) as an MP3
file. In Audacity, go to File > Export Audio... Save
the file with the name of the podcast episode as
you did the Audacity Project (e.g., *055_episode_
podcast_trends*). You should save this file in the
folder *published*. When you export your file to
an MP3 file, Audacity will give you the option of
adding in metadata for your episode. Metadata is
the description of your podcast (see Figure 3.8)
that allows your podcast to show up in searches.
iTunes (and other aggregators; more about these
later in the chapter) uses these data to categorize
the podcast, which then allows it to show up in
the iTunes Store search and in its browse functions.
We suggest that you keep the metadata consistent
from episode to episode—there are elements like
the Track Title and Track Number you will need to
update, however.

● As a side note, while you could keep your audio
file as an M4A, we suggest that you change it to an
MP3 because it will increase the number of devices
on which the file can be played.

Figure 3.5 Example 1 of Raw M4A Audio File Opened in Audacity

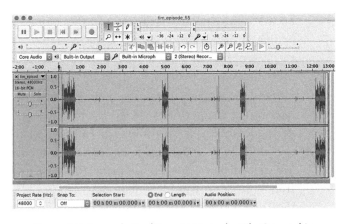

Figure 3.6 Example 2 of Raw M4A Audio File Opened in Audacity

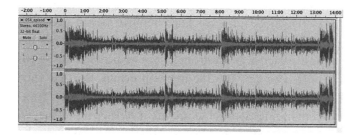

Figure 3.7 Example of Finished Audio for an Episode

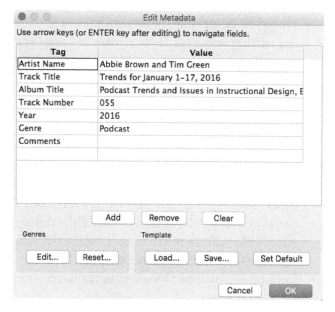

Figure 3.8 Example of Metadata to Include for Each Podcast
Episode

4. **Add Bumpers.** The next step is to add in the bumpers to this file. Tim opens both bumper files in Audacity. He copies the audio from the beginning bumper file and pastes it at the front of the audio file that he exported as an MP3 file in the previous step. He then completes the same process for the ending bumper—copying the audio and adding it to the end of the file he exported in the previous step. Tim then saves the file. The entire audio for the episode is now in one audio file.

- As a reminder, earlier in the chapter we suggested that you create your bumpers ahead of time because they will most likely remain the same from episode to episode. When Abbie created our bumpers, he saved them as MP3 files.

5. **Edit Audio Quality.** At this point in the process, Tim will make any necessary adjustments to the audio quality.

- The first edit we suggest is to *level* or *normalize* the audio. This process takes the entire audio file and makes the volume consistent. With multiple audio files being pasted into one file (as was done in steps 3 and 4), the volume levels of the different audio files will not be the same. Leveling the audio, as mentioned, makes it consistent. In Audacity, this can be accomplished by going to the menu option Effect > Leveler.

- The second edit we suggest is to adjust the bass volume of the audio. This is not always necessary. We occasionally increase the bass of the entire audio because we believe that it gives it a better quality sound. This is a personal preference, and you will have to determine if it is necessary or helpful for your recording. In Audacity, increasing the bass can be accomplished by going to the menu option Effect > Bass and Treble. You will want to experiment with different bass levels to achieve optimal sound quality.

● It is important to note that we are not audio experts. While we have found that these two edit options work best for us, we understand that there are other edits that might enhance the audio quality even more.

6. **Test MP3 File.** Although Tim goes through the entire audio file during the editing steps, he tests the MP3 file one final time.

● Tim saves the final MP3 audio file one final time. He saves the file again as an Audacity Project. He uses the same file name used in step 3 (Edit the Content). The Audacity Project will be the same as the name of the podcast episode (e.g., *055_episode_podcast_trends*). Audacity will ask if you want to save over the previous version of the project; you can save over the previous version. Saving the project at this point in the process allows you to come back to the complete episode file to make any necessary adjustments, if needed.

● Tim looks over the entire audio file (Figure 3.7) to visually determine if the entire audio file is intact. He then closes Audacity after the MP3 file and the Audacity Project have been saved.

- Tim opens the MP3 file in QuickTime (or it can be opened in iTunes) to ensure that it opens and plays successfully.

Distributing the Podcast

If you have been following along and completing the steps outlined in this chapter, you could have a complete podcast episode at this point. Technically, however, it would not be a podcast until the episode audio file has been distributed—that is, published. You could still share the episode audio file with individuals, but it is not a podcast until is it is made publicly available through an established distribution system. Publishing means making the MP3 file available on the internet in a format that allows podcast software like iTunes or TuneIn to distribute it through syndication via an RSS feed, making the audio and show notes available to listeners using a podcast client like an iPhone or Android device.

You might be scratching your head right now wondering what this all truly means. We do not blame you if you are. It can be confusing initially, but the good news is that you do not have to understand the technical aspects of what is going on in order to get your podcast into syndication. What you will need is space on the internet where you store your podcast episodes (the MP3 files). You will also need a website where your podcast RSS feed is hosted. Finally, you will need to submit your podcast to iTunes for it to be syndicated. Once it is listed on iTunes, others will be able to find it and subscribe to it.

While other podcast directories exist where you can get your podcast listed and have it syndicated, iTunes is by far the largest and most popular. As such, we provide the process necessary for you to get it listed with iTunes. This is the approach we took—we made certain we did what we needed to get listed in iTunes. Once we had it listed in iTunes, we knew it would be ready for virtually all other podcast directories.

Hosting

Before sharing the steps we use to publish podcast episodes (see section *Step 3 Publishing: Making the Podcast Available to the World*), we need to first discuss hosting a podcast. There are two general elements to hosting a podcast. These two elements will allow you to get your podcast into syndication and publish your podcast episodes. One element is to secure internet space where you can maintain a website that includes your podcast RSS feed. The other element is to secure internet storage space for the MP3 files that you create for your podcast episodes. It is important to note that once you accomplish these two elements you will not have to do them for every episode. Let's explore how we have accomplished these elements for our *Trends and Issues* podcast.

WEBSITE FOR HOSTING THE PODCAST RSS FEED

Our podcast website uses the open-source content management system WordPress (www.wordpress.com/). WordPress originally began as a blogging platform in 2003, but since that time has grown into a robust platform that allows for more than blogging sites. While there are a number of options available for creating a site to host your podcast RSS feed, we chose the WordPress platform for the following reasons.

1. It is a stable platform. It has developed a vibrant and growing development community over the years. As such, the WordPress platform is well maintained with regular updates occurring to make certain that the platform operates without issues.

2. You are able to host a podcast RSS feed through WordPress.

    ● As we discussed earlier in the chapter, what makes a podcast truly a podcast—rather than simply audio files—is syndication. As a reminder, syndication is the process that allows a listener to subscribe to a podcast once, and continue to automatically receive new episodes of the podcast through sources like iTunes when new episodes are published. The key to syndication is the podcast RSS feed.

    ● A podcast RSS feed is similar to a basic webpage, but it is formatted using XML rather than HTML. An XML-formatted document is not, however, designed for viewing like a webpage created using HTML; in fact, the only internet browser that will display an XML-formatted document in a readable format is Firefox. If you were to view a podcast RSS feed in Firefox it would list information about a podcast's episodes with the most recent episode listed at the top (see Figure 3.9).

- You must have a podcast RSS feed for your podcast to be listed in iTunes (and other podcast directories).

3. It is important to note that you do not need to understand the technical aspects of how an RSS feed is created. You are able to create your podcast RSS feed using WordPress. Our podcast feed is www.trendsandissues.com/feed. Yours will follow a similar format: www.yourdomainname.com/feed.

4. Blubrry, the company we use—and suggest that you use—to store podcast audio files works seamlessly with the WordPress platform. The integration of Blubrry and WordPress is accomplished through the PowerPress plugin (see section below *Activating and Connecting PowerPress*). This plugin allows our podcast episodes to be played directly on our site. PowerPress also assists you in getting your podcast submitted to iTunes (see section below on *Submitting to iTunes*).

- Figure 3.9 shows an example of show notes of one of our podcast episodes that is located on our website that uses WordPress. You can see the PowerPress media player located at the bottom of the show notes. A listener could listen to our podcast directly on our website or download a copy of the audio file to listen to using different software.

5. WordPress provides tools that allow an individual to create a site without needing web design and development

skills. While we have skill in web design and development, we appreciate that we are able to easily make changes to our site without a great deal of effort. You will be surprised to see how quickly you can create a functional and visually well-designed website using WordPress, even if you do not have web design and development experience.

6. WordPress is an expandable platform; that is, it is designed to allow for features to be added easily to a site through the use of widgets and plugins. Widgets primarily allow you to structure the layout, design, and navigation of your site. Plugins bring added functionality to a website. As we mentioned, we use the Power-Press plugin on our WordPress site.

We, like millions of others, appreciate that WordPress provides its users with the ability to create a free website through its web servers. You can accomplish this by going to www.wordpress.com/. While this is something we appreciate, there is a major limitation with going this route. You are not able to install plugins when you create a free WordPress site that is hosted on a WordPress server. You will need to use a web hosting company that allows installation of the WordPress platform. This will allow you to use the PowerPress plugin along with other plugins designed for WordPress.

- We use the web hosting company BlueHost (www. bluehost.com/) because of its reliability, cost, and ease of setting up a site using the WordPress platform. As of the writing of this book, we pay $12 a month.

● The other cost you will need to incur is for a domain name for your website. This cost is a yearly fee that depends on the type of domain name (e.g., .com) that you purchase. We pay $15 a year for our domain name www.trendsandissues.com/. We suggest you purchase the domain name directly through Bluehost. Doing so saves you the step of having to map your domain name to the Bluehost web servers.

● Once you have your account with Bluehost and your domain name purchased, your next step is to install the WordPress platform for your site. You do this directly in Bluehost. You will need to locate the *Install WordPress* option when you are logged into Bluehost. Bluehost walks you through the installation process, or you could pay Bluehost to install WordPress for you. We did the install process on our own, and we found it was not difficult because you are step-by-step walked through the installation process. It is highly important that you go through the process methodically and deliberately (in other words, read directions and prompts before clicking buttons).

● Once the installation process is complete—about 15 min—you will be able to log in to your site. Make certain that you remember your username and password. The URL to log in will include your domain name followed by /wp-login.php. Our login URL, for example, is http://trendsandissues. com/wp-login.php. This URL is how we log in to access our podcast site that is using the WordPress platform (Figure 3.10).

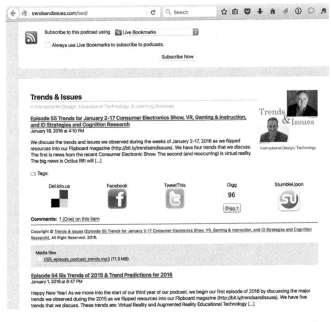

Figure 3.9 Podcast RSS Feed Displayed on the Firefox Web Browser

Storing MP3 Files

Our podcast MP3 files (i.e., episodes) are hosted, as we have mentioned, with a media hosting service called Blubrry (www.blubrry.com/). While we considered using free options for storing our MP3 files on the internet, we chose Blubrry because of the services it provides and its ease of use. As we mentioned, Blubrry seamlessly integrates with WordPress through a plugin called Power-Press. This is important because WordPress is where we host our podcast RSS feed (as we described in the section

Episode 55 Trends for January 2-17 Consumer Electronics Show, VR, Gaming & Instruction, and ID Strategies and Cognition Research

Image from htt://onforb.es/1n6Xfwr

We discuss the trends and issues we observed during the weeks of January 2-17, 2016 as we flipped resources into our Flipboard magazine (http://bit.ly/trendsandissues). We have four trends that we discuss. The first is news from the recent **Consumer Electronic Show.** The second (and reoccurring) is **virtual reality**. The big news is Octlus Rift will ship in July of this year. The third was a focus on **gaming** related to instruction and cognitive development. The fourth trend is a mixture of resources on **instructional design strategies** and **cognition research**.

We have four recommended readings for the week.

- 48 Books to Add to Your Tech Reading List for 2016 by Cameron Chapman http://skill-crush.com/2016/01/05/48-books-to-add-to-your-tech-reading-list-for-2016/
- Patenting Pedagogy? Experts attempt to make sense of Khan Academy's patent application for A/B testing in education — and whether it can even be patented. by Carl Strausheim https://www.insidehighered.com/news/2016/01/15/explaining-khan-academys-patent-application-ab-testing-education
- Can Computer Games Improve the Ability to Study by University of Bristol http://www.bris.ac.uk/education/news/2016/computer-games.html
- CES Roundup: Have We Discovered Anything New in 2016 by Brad Auerbach http://www.forbes.com/sites/bradauerbach/2016/01/10/ces-roundup-have-we-discovered-anything-new-in-2016/#2715e4857a0b6884b316668d

To cite the Trends & Issues podcast:

Brown, A. & Green, T. (Producers). (2016, January 18). *Trends and Issues in Instructional Design, Educational Technology, and Learning Sciences* [Audio Podcast]. Retrieved from http://trendsandissues.com/

Our next podcast episode will be February 1, 2016

Podcast: Play in new window | Download

Figure 3.10 Podcast Episode Show Notes Example with PowerPress Media Player

Website for Hosting the Podcast RSS Feed). As of the writing of this book, we pay $12 a month for Blubrry, and the price has remained the same since we started using it in December 2013.

Visit www.blubrry.com/ to sign up for Blubrry's media hosting. When you create a username and password, you will be directed to add your podcast show title (program title) and create an internet-friendly URL (i.e., Web address); you will be provided instructions on how to create an internet-friendly URL. You will also need to put in your payment information for the monthly storage cost. You will only need the 100 MB storage space, which is the least expensive option. Once you have your account set up, you will now need to connect it with your WordPress site. Let's discuss how this is accomplished.

Activating and Connecting PowerPress

Possibly the most complicated aspect of hosting your podcast is connecting your Blubrry account (through the PowerPress plugin) with your WordPress site that you set up with Bluehost. The process is complicated because there are a number of steps that need to be taken in a specific order for it to work correctly. The good news is that you will only need to go through this process once.

- Before we discuss the steps, let's outline the two primary reasons we need to connect the two together. The first is to set up your podcast to be accepted in iTunes. You will be walked through this process when you activate the PowerPress plugin on your WordPress site. The second is to have your podcast audio files accessible and playable directly on your WordPress site. In general, activating PowerPress on your site makes your podcast accessible in two ways—through syndication in iTunes and directly on your website.

● The first step in activating PowerPress is to log in to your WordPress site (as a reminder, ours is www. trendsandsissues.com/wp-login.php—yours will follow a similar pattern).

● Once you are logged in, you will need to go to the *Dashboard*. The dashboard is the area that allows you to make changes to your site. Figure 3.11 shows an example of what a typical WordPress site dashboard looks like.

● On the dashboard, locate the *Plugins* menu. Click on this menu to find *Add New*. This will bring up a new screen. Find the *Search Plugins* search box—it should be up near the top right of the screen. Type in "powerpress" in the search box. Several plugin options will appear. Find the one that reads *Blubrry PowerPress Podcasting plugin* (see Figure 3.12).

● You are now ready to install. Click on the *Install Now* button (see Figure 3.12). You will be taken to a different screen and the PowerPress plugin will now install. Once it installs, click on *Activate the Plugin*.

● You are now ready to configure PowerPress. On your screen, you should see an image that looks like Figure 3.13. You want to click on the *Settings* option.

You will be taken to another screen that allows you to configure PowerPress (see Figure 3.14).

● As you can see in Figure 3.14, you will be led through the configuration process. There are three major steps. From this point on, you will need to follow the prompts. The information you need to include is specific to your Blubrry account and your podcast.

Submitting Your Podcast to the iTunes Directory

The last step (#3) in the configuration process of PowerPress (see Figure 3.14) is submitting your podcast to iTunes for it to be listed in its directory. We especially appreciate this option being provided through the PowerPress plugin because the process is streamlined. There are a few things to be aware of when submitting your podcast to iTunes. The first is that the acceptance process for iTunes may take a week or more, and you may have your podcast rejected if you do not follow iTunes' guidelines. Apple will notify you through the email you provided when you submit your podcast for acceptance into the iTunes directory. The second is that you will need to produce at least one podcast episode and one blog post associated with your podcast prior to submitting to iTunes. Step 2 of activating PowerPress will walk you through creating a blog post, if you are not familiar with how to do this. Step 3 is that you will need your podcast artwork created that follows iTunes' standards.

● If you need more information about PowerPress, you can visit http://create.blubrry.com/resources/powerpress/.

Figure 3.11 Example of the Dashboard Menu for a
WordPress Site

Blubrry PowerPress Podcasting plugin

Install Now

More Details

No. 1 Podcasting plugin
for WordPress, with
simple & advanced
modes, players,
subscribe tools, and
more! Supports iTunes,
Google Play, Stitcher...

By Blubrry

Figure 3.12 The Blubrry PowerPress Podcasting Plugin
Installation Screen in WordPress

☐ **Blubrry PowerPress**
Deactivate | Edit | Settings

Blubrry PowerPress is the No. 1 Podcasting plugin for WordPress. Developed by podcasters for podcasters; features include Simple and Advanced modes, multiple audio/video player options, subscribe to podcast tools, podcast SEO features, and more! Fully supports iTunes, Google Play, Stitcher, and Blubrry Podcasting directories, as well as all podcast applications and clients.

Version 6.3.1 | By Blubrry | View details

Figure 3.13 Finding the Settings to Configure PowerPress

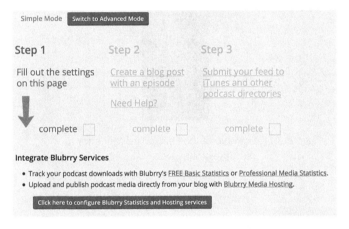

Figure 3.14 Configure Screen for PowerPress

Publishing: Making the Podcast Available to the World

We are going to assume that you have completed all of the elements described in the *Hosting* section of this chapter. This means you have your podcast website created using WordPress; you have secured media hosting using Blubrry; you have integrated Blubrry with your WordPress site using the PowerPress plugin; you have successfully configured PowerPress; and, finally, your podcast has been accepted and listed in the iTunes directory. You are now at the point where you can publish your podcast episodes. In essence, you are ready to make them available to the world through iTunes and on your website.

There are three general steps that we complete to publish a podcast episode. The first is to upload the completed podcast episode audio file to Blubrry. The second is to create a blog post using the show notes for an episode. The third is to embed the podcast episode audio file directly in our blog post for the episode. Let's explore these three steps.

1. **Uploading Podcast Episode Audio to Blubrry.** Once Tim has the final version of the audio file (MP3) for an episode, he uploads it to Blubrry. The audio file must be in Blubrry for iTunes to locate the episode and include it in its directory. Additionally, the audio file needs to be in Blubrry for it to be embedded in the blog post for the episode (see step 3 below *Embedding Episode Audio File*).

   ● Tim logs into Blubrry. He clicks on the *Podcaster Dashboard* located at the top right of the page. This brings up a set of menus that can be selected.

   ● Tim clicks on *Upload New Media Files* located under Podcast Hosting. He follows the prompts to upload the episode MP3 file. Once the file has been uploaded, the *Make Public* option for the file must be clicked. Until this is selected, the audio file will not be available to iTunes or for embedding in a blog post.

   ● It is important to note that from the time when the file is made public to it showing up in iTunes could take several hours.

- Technically, once the file is available in iTunes, the podcast episode is downloadable. Steps 2 and 3 are not necessary for the episode to be made available. However, these steps provide listeners with another option for accessing our podcast audio. The blog posts also provide an alternative way for listeners to find out about our podcast.

2. **Creating a Blog Post Using Show Notes.** Show notes provide a summary of the major topics that we cover in an episode. We turn our show notes for an episode into a blog post on our website. Figure 3.10 shows an example of a blog post that includes show notes for episode 55 of our podcast.

   - Tim maintains our website. He is responsible for taking the show notes and creating a blog post for each episode we produce. The show notes primarily come from the conversation we have prior to recording an episode. We discuss this above in the *Pre-Recording* section of this chapter.

   - Each blog post for an episode follows the same pattern. We include an image. We include a brief summary of the trends we discussed in the episode. We list our recommended readings include the URLs where the readings can be accessed. We include the citation that can be used to cite the podcast episode. We embed the audio for the episode.

   - Tim logs in to our website to create a blog post. In the dashboard, he selects Post > Add New to create the new blog post. This will bring up a template where Tim includes the title of the blog post, the text (show notes), and an image. Tim will save the blog post as a *draft*.

3. **Embedding Episode Audio File.** The PowerPress plugin provides an option for embedding an episode audio file in a blog post that can be played through its media player. We use this option because it allows for our episode audio files to be played directly from our website. We include this for each episode blog post.

- To accomplish this task, Tim accesses the blog post template for the podcast episode where the audio will be embedded. He goes to Posts > All Posts and then clicks on the title of the blog post. This brings up the blog post for editing.

- Tim scrolls down near the bottom of the blog post template to locate the *Podcast Episode* menu. Figure 3.15 shows an example of what this menu looks like.

- Tim clicks on the *Link to Media hosted on Blubrry. com* button to access the podcast episode audio file to embed. Figure 3.16 shows an example of what this looks like. Tim clicks *select* for the audio file he wants to embed.

- Once the audio file is selected, the URL for where that media file is located on Blubrry.com shows up next to the *Media URL* (see Figure 3.15).

- At this point in the process, the entire blog post is ready to go live to the world. Tim scrolls up to the top of the blog post template to the *Publish* menu. He first clicks on the *Preview* button to test out the blog post. Clicking on *Preview* opens up a new browser window that displays what the blog post will look like when it is made public. The blog post will be active. Tim tests out the links and then the audio by playing it through the PowerPress media player located at the bottom of the blog post.

● Once he is satisfied that the blog post is ready to go, Tim closes the browser window (or tab) of the preview in order to get back to the blog post template. He then clicks *Publish* to make the blog post for the episode live to the world (Figure 3.17).

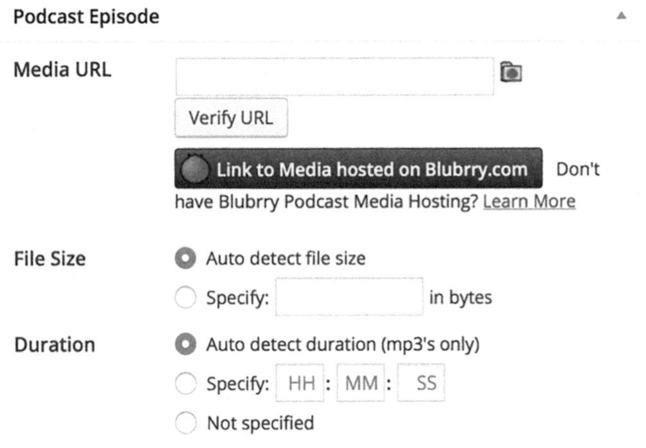

Podcast Episode   ▲

Media URL   [   ] 📷

                   [Verify URL]

                   [🔘 **Link to Media hosted on Blubrry.com**] Don't
                   have Blubrry Podcast Media Hosting? Learn More

File Size   🔘 Auto detect file size

                   ⚪ Specify: [   ] in bytes

Duration   🔘 Auto detect duration (mp3's only)

                   ⚪ Specify: [HH] : [MM] : [SS]

                   ⚪ Not specified

Figure 3.15 Menu for Embedding Podcast Audio into a Blog Post on WordPress

Blubrry Podcast Hosting

Select Media

Select from media files uploaded to blubrry.com: Upload Media File

Last 20 Published media files:

055_episode_podcast_trends.mp3 *11.3MB*
· Published on January 19, 2016   Select

054_episode_podcast_trendsandissues.mp3 *12.8MB*
· Published on January 2, 2016   Select

053_episode_podcast.mp3 *9.6MB*
· Published on December 23, 2015   Select

052_episode_podcast.mp3 *10.0MB*
· Published on December 7, 2015   Select

051_episode_final.mp3 *5.5MB*
· Published on November 25, 2015   Select

050_episode_podcast_trends_final.mp3 *19.3MB*
· Published on November 11, 2015   Select

049_podcast_trendsandissues_browngreen.mp3 *9.1MB*
· Published on October 27, 2015   Select

048_episode.mp3 *7.8MB*   Select

Figure 3.16 List of Media to Select to Embed in a Blog Post
after Clicking on the Link to Media hosted on
Blubrry.com Button

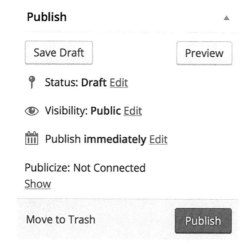

Figure 3.17 Menu for Making a Blog Post Live to the World

Summary

You should have an overall understanding of how to produce a podcast now that you have made it through this chapter. It is important to keep in mind, as we mentioned in the chapter opening, that the process we have outlined is our specific process that we have refined as we produced over 75 podcast episodes. If you follow the process we have outlined, you will be able to produce a high-quality OER podcast. We know that it will take time, patience, and persistence the first few times you go through this process. We believe, however, you will experience a great deal of satisfaction when you see and hear your podcast once you do. You will also gain skills that will allow you to create other audio OERs.

4 | Digital Text

Text is one of our oldest forms of instructional media. The earliest examples of writing date back to around 3100 BCE in ancient Sumer, where cuneiform marks were inscribed on clay tablets. Egyptians developed their own writing script about a century later, writing on papyrus sheets (American Printing History Association, n.d.; Gascoigne, 2001). As forms of writing have evolved over the past 5,000 years, so has the method in which text is stored and presented.

We are all familiar with books, booklets, posters, and magazines printed on paper. Print media is an important part of most classroom instruction and study. We tend to equate the written word with education, and our language reflects this with idiomatic expressions like "hitting the books," which refers to studying. With the advent of networked computing, text has evolved further. A great deal of the text we use today is digital, stored as files on a computer drive, and presented on screens that range in size from traditional computer monitors to handheld tablets, e-readers, and smartphones.

Distribution and Access

Digital text documents offer a number of advantages over traditional, paper-printed documents. Digital text can be duplicated and distributed a seemingly infinite number of times while maintaining its original quality. The size display of digital text can be adjusted to the needs of the individual (often this means enlarging the text to make it easier to read for people with vision challenges). Digital files are relatively small and can be easily transmitted over networks such as the internet and stored in great numbers on devices such as e-readers. While traditional, printed text has its own advantages, the greatest being that it does not require a digital device on which to read it, digital text's benefits in terms of ease of distribution through available networks make it an excellent open educational resource option.

Text Basics

Digital text is a computer-based representation of traditional printing. In general, print is comprised of letters, numbers, and punctuation marks used in combination to convey information. These letters, numbers, and punctuation marks are generally organized by size and style. Text size is usually measured in points or em size. There are approximately 72 points to an inch, and the size of a font or type is the size required to render the characters within a rectangle referred to as an em by print designers (Butterick, 2016).

There are four general categories of font or type style. Each style has its own uses in designing easy-to-read and appealing documents:

Serif: The characters have little marks (serifs) incorporated into their design. Times is a popular serif font. Serif marks generally make reading easier and serif fonts are often used as body text.

Sans-Serif: The characters are "plain" with no serif marks. Helvetica is a popular sans-serif font. Sans-serif fonts tend to look modern and minimalist. They are often used in business presentations and make excellent heading text.

Decorative: The characters are designed with extreme features. These are intended to evoke a mood or feeling. Tombstone and Apple's San Francisco are examples of decorative fonts. These are generally more difficult to read and are used sparingly to gain the reader's immediate attention.

Script: The characters are derived from writing and calligraphy. Popular examples are Marker Felt and Apple Chancery. These are generally used as decorative fonts or to create the look of a hand-written document.

For more about font and type styles, see the Type Classifications page (Haley, n.d.) at fonts.com.

How to: PDF Files

PDF (Portable Document Format) files are an excellent method of sharing text. They are easy to create and equally easy to access from just about any digital device. PDF was originally developed by Adobe Systems and is currently an open standard maintained by the International Organization for Standardization (Adobe Systems, Incorporated, 2016). PDF files are a reliable means of presenting documents that look the same no matter what combination of software and hardware is used to view them.

You can create a PDF file using most word-processing, graphics-manipulation, and desktop-publishing software. Essentially, any handout, flyer, news article, reading, or assignment that you create using software such as Microsoft Word or Google Docs can be saved and distributed as a PDF file. As an example, let's look at the steps involved in creating a PDF file using Google Docs:

1. Start a new document in Google Docs. This requires a Google account; if you do not currently have an account you can sign up for an individual Google account for free (see https://accounts.google.com/signup).

2. Create your text presentation using the editing tools (Figure 4.1).

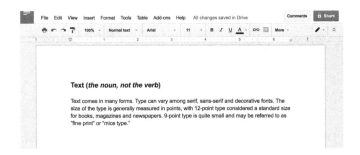

Figure 4.1 A Google Docs file
Source: Google and the Google logo are registered trademarks of Google Inc., used with permission.

3. Save your Google Docs work as a PDF by clicking File → Download as → PDF Document (.pdf) (Figure 4.2).

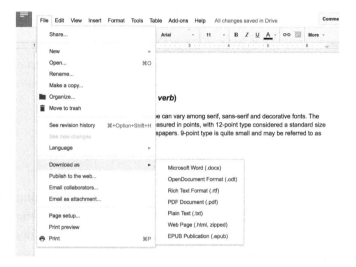

Figure 4.2 Saving a Google Doc file as a PDF file
Source: Google and the Google logo are registered trademarks of Google Inc., used with permission.

4. Once you have downloaded the file as a PDF you can distribute the file over any digital network such the internet, e-mail, or social media. It can be opened and read on most devices. You can upload the file into a social media feed such as Facebook or Instagram by adding the file to a post, and of course you can attach a PDF file to e-mail messages. You can also make your Google Doc publicly available so that you do not have to download and redistribute the file itself.

5. Using Google Docs, you can make a PDF file publicly available by selecting the Publish to the Web option

under File. By selecting Publish to the Web, you make your Google Doc file publicly viewable and Google Docs will provide you with a link you can share.

PDF files can include images, links, audio, video, form fields, and other interactive elements. Bear in mind that the downloadable file increases in size dramatically with the addition of audio or video.

eBooks

An eBook is an electronic book. It is published in digital format that can be read using devices including desktop and laptop computers, tablets, and smartphones. PDF files can be viewed with e-reading devices such as the Amazon Kindle. It takes a bit more planning to create a nice-looking eBook using PDF, but mostly because books tend to be larger and more elaborate than most other text forms. Most professionally-produced eBooks are files other than PDF such as ePub, but PDF works quite well to get started.

eBooks use the same format as traditional books, and readers expect a similar experience that includes the sense of turning pages, using bookmarks, page numbering, and division of content into chapters, as well as standard publication information such as copyright, authorship, date of publication, and ISBN (International Standard Book Number: a unique identifier). You are not required to include all of these things in an eBook, but you should be aware that readers have come to expect them as part of the overall format, especially if they intend to cite your work.

How to: Blogging

The word blog is derived from "web log." It is a website where a person or group shares information in periodic installments. The posting schedule is up to the individual or group; some blogs are updated monthly (or less) while others are updated multiple times each day. Blogging can be a great way to freely share your ideas with others. Since blogs are web based, they can be accessed worldwide using any browser tool.

Getting started with blogging is relatively easy. However, maintaining the blog with regular updates can prove challenging. Running a blog is similar to keeping a public journal or diary; it takes a bit of discipline to add to your blog with regularity. You do not have to maintain the blog forever, though. Like any "serial" media (that is, anything with episodes), you can choose to end the run at any time.

A blog is basically a website that is designed for frequent updates. There are a number of free and fee-based blog options available, and most are very easy to use. One of the major differences between free and fee-based options is the domain name of your blog. Premium options allow you to decide the exact name (for example, mygreat-blog.com) while free options generally limit you to using a version of their domain name (something like mygreat-blog.wordpress.com). Free options may also include advertising that you cannot completely control while fee-based options provide you with complete control over all visible content. Free blog options may also limit the number of viewers allowed per month (though, it is usually a pretty large number allowed).

We keep a blog, trendsandissues.com, on the latest educational technology news (see Figure 4.3). Our blog serves as home base for our podcasting and other social media activities. It looks pretty sophisticated, but it actually is pretty easy to set up and maintain because the trickier aspects of the coding and design are taken care of by the host service (which for us is Wordpress).

Wordpress (wordpress.com) is by far the most popular blogging software. The Wordpress site will guide you through the steps of creating your own blog and offers both a free option and a "premium" subscription option.

Figure 4.3 Screenshot of our blog

Other easy-to-use, free blogging options include Tumblr (tumblr.com) and Blogger (blogger.com). Like Wordpress, Blogger and Tumblr guide you through the steps of starting a blog as soon as you arrive at their home site.

Summary

Though it is so common that we often take it for granted, text is a medium all its own. We have been refining text design and delivery for thousands of years. We suspect the ancient Sumerians would be quite amazed at the improvements made over their wedge-shaped marks in clay tablets! Digital text is a relatively easy-to-produce and distribute open educational resource. Text files can be quite small and therefore particularly easy to distribute, and most educators are well versed in the use of documents for instructional purposes.

PDF files and blogging are a great way to use text as an open resource. PDF files are easy to read on almost any digital device, and blogging is a web-based format that is equally easy to read and distribute. PDF files are particularly good for sharing reproducible content such as handouts and lesson plans, while blogging lends itself to episodic or serial content such as monthly articles. PDFs and blogs can include more elaborate media as well such as audio and video, but it's important to keep in mind that adding media can create challenges in distributing the work due to large file sizes.

5 | Curated Digital Media

An interesting infographic titled *Data Never Sleeps 4.0* (Domo, 2016) highlights the amount of activity and information that is generated every minute on the internet. The amount of activity and information generated is staggering! The infographic indicates, for example, that every minute 400 hours of new video are shared on YouTube and 9,678 tweets are sent. Granted, not all of the information shared on the internet is valid or reliable—thus, there is the need for individuals to have the ability to effectively sift through the information to organize and share it in ways that are meaningful. One approach to accomplish this is digital curation. Rosenbaum (2011) wrote that "Curation is about selection, organization, presentation, and evolution. While computers can aggregate content, information, or any shape or size of data, aggregation without curation is just a big pile of stuff that seems related but lacks a qualitative organization" (p. 4). In this chapter, we discuss how to use three different tools to create open educational resources (OERs) consisting of curated digital media.

How to Curate Digital Media

The primary tasks to consider when curating digital media are *collecting* the digital media, *organizing* it in a meaningful way, and *sharing* it with others. There are a number of different tools that allow you to accomplish these tasks in order to curate digital media. We focus on three tools that allow you to collect, organize, and share digital media in different ways. We have selected these specific tools for the following reasons: (1) the tools provide distinct methods for curating media; (2) the tools are stable, and they have been around for at least 5 years; and (3) the tools are cross-platform. RSS Feeds, Flipboard, and Storify are the tools we describe and provide guidelines on for creating your own curated digital media that can be turned into OERs.

Rich Site Summary/Really Simple Syndication

One straightforward method for curating digital media is to use tools that take advantage of RSS—rich site summary or really simple syndication, as it is often called. RSS is a type of web syndication that allows content from one website to be available on other sites or applications. The content is provided as either a summary or full version of the website content using standardized formats like an XML file that includes specific metadata such as a summary of the content, the content author's name, and the date the content was published. This standardized format allows for a cross-platform RSS document to be created that is called a *feed* or *RSS feed*.

An RSS feed allows an individual to subscribe to a website through the feed (see Figure 5.1) in order to receive new content automatically rather than having to manually visit the website for new content. The new content is received and viewed through a tool such as an RSS reader or aggregator. These tools will automatically monitor websites a user has subscribed to and make the content available when an RSS reader or aggregator is used. Figure 5.1 is what a typical icon looks like that you will find on a website that has an RSS available. Figure 5.2 shows the RSS feed icon on a website. Clicking on the icon would allow an individual to subscribe to the blog in order to receive automatic updates to the content.

Curating RSS Feeds Using Feedly

Feedly (www.feedly.com) is an example of an aggregator. Feedly allows a user to create collections of

Figure 5.1 RSS feed icon. This image is an example of the icon typically used to signify an RSS feed. Image adapted by the authors from https://en.wikipedia. org/wiki/RSS#/media/File:Feed-icon.svg

Source: Adapted by Tim Green, PhD.

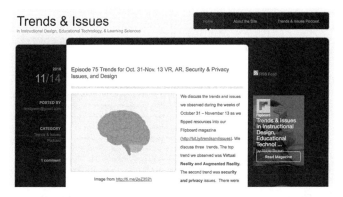

Figure 5.2 Subscribing to an RSS feed. This figure illustrates what a link to subscribe to an RSS feed on a website looks like. Site is from http://trendsandissues.com, an example of an OER (a blog for a podcast) created and produced by the authors

information from various websites by subscribing to RSS feeds from these websites. Figure 5.3 illustrates what content looks like when RSS feeds collect content from websites and then bring this content into Feedly to be displayed and viewed by the user. Figure 5.3 is a collection of content from RSS feeds from various websites focusing on the topics of instructional design, educational technology, and learning sciences. One would click on the various links in the content collection to view the website content.

You will need a Feedly account to create a collection. While you can create collections in Feedly with a free basic account, you will need a paid account to share these collections.

Figure 5.3 A Feedly feed collection. This figure illustrates what an RSS feed collection looks like using the feed aggregation tool Feedly. The example is from one of the author's personal feed collections

1. Once you are logged in to Feedly, you will see a screen that looks similar to the one in Figure 5.4. Click on the menu icon—the three lines at the top left of the screen. After clicking on the menu icon, you will see several choices appear (see Figure 5.5).

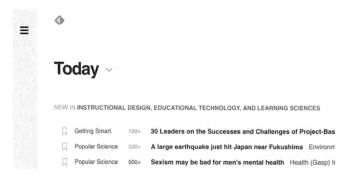

Figure 5.4 Feedly screen when logged in. This is an example of what the screen looks like when logged in to a Feedly account

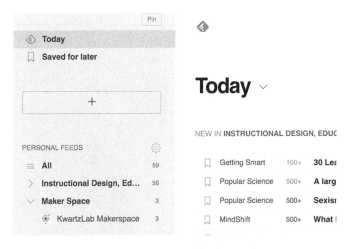

Figure 5.5 Feedly menu screen. This figure illustrates an example of the screen you will get after clicking on the menu icon

2. Click on the button that includes the + sign on it. This will bring up another screen (see Figure 5.6) where you can start adding feeds to your collection. You have several options of information to enter to find feeds that you would like to add to your collection. As an example, we used the hashtag #stem to find resources that focus on STEM education. Figure 5.7 shows the first three resources that came up. You can see from looking at the three choices that not all of them focus on STEM education.

3. When you find a feed you want to add to your collection, click on the FOLLOW button. This will bring up another screen (see Figure 5.8) that will allow the feed to be added to a collection.

Figure 5.6 Adding feeds screen. This figure illustrates how to add feeds to a collection in Feedly

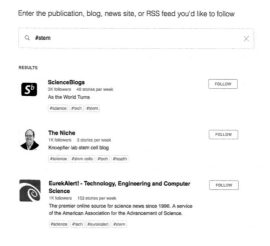

Figure 5.7 Feed search results. This figure illustrates the first three feeds that came up when using the hashtag #stem to search for feeds on STEM education

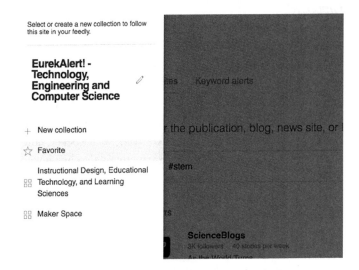

Figure 5.8 Adding a feed to a collection. This figure illustrates how to add a feed to a collection

4. You have two options when you are at the screen (Figure 5.8) to add the feed to a collection: (1) create a new collection by clicking on the New collection link or (2) add the feed to an existing collecting by clicking on the name of the collection. Figure 5.8 shows two existing collections *Instructional Design, Educational Technology, and Learning Sciences* and *Maker Space.*

Once a collection is created, it can be shared through a unique internet address that is generated by Feedly. As we mentioned, you have to have a paid account to share a collection in order to make it an OER. You can view a Feedly OER on instructional design, educational technology, and learning sciences by visiting http://feedly.com/theedtechdoctor/Educational%20Technology.

Flipboard

Flipboard is primarily an app-based tool that provides users with a platform to create and view digital magazines from various social media tools and web-based media. A user interacts with *Flipboard* by "flipping" through aggregated media displayed in a digital magazine format. While it is available for iOS, Android, Blackberry, and Windows devices, *Flipboard* magazines can also be viewed through most internet browsers.

To get a sense of what a *Flipboard* magazine looks like, we suggest visiting our magazine—*Trends and Issues in Instructional Design, Educational Technology, and Learning Sciences*—at http://bit.ly/trendsandissues. Figure 5.9 is a screenshot of the cover of our magazine as viewed through an internet browser. On the screenshot, several different elements about a *Flipboard* magazine are

Figure 5.9 Screen shot of a *Flipboard* magazine. The image illustrates different aspects of a *Flipboard* magazine cover page

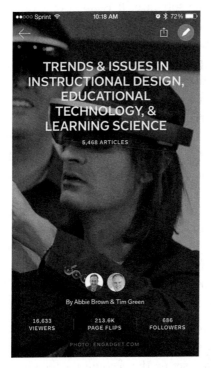

Figure 5.10 Screen shot of a *Flipboard* magazine. The image
illustrates the cover of a *Flipboard* magazine as
viewed on an iOS mobile device

highlighted and described to give you an orientation to a
Flipboard magazine (Figure 5.10).

Curating a Digital Magazine Using Flipboard

The following guide will help step you through creating a
Flipboard magazine of curated digital media that can become
an OER. The steps provided are those from the internet

version of the software. It is important to note that the mobile app has similar steps, but it may vary slightly. It is also important to note that the steps to creating a magazine could change as *Flipboard* releases software updates. We can report that since we have been using the tool, the process for creating a magazine has remained relatively similar. Finally, we provide screenshots that include descriptions of various elements. We do not point out all elements that you will see on the screenshot—only the ones we feel are necessary to understand how to create a *Flipboard* magazine.

1. Sign up for a free account at www.flipboard.com. You will need to follow the required tasks to complete your account (e.g., follow various *Flipboard* magazine topics, verify your account through your email). Once you have completed these steps, you will be able to create your own magazine.

2. Click on the **profile** button at the top right. It will be a circle with your first initial of the name you included when you set up the account (or the image you added for your profile). When you click on this button, you will be taken to a screen (see Figure 5.11) where you can create a new magazine.

3. While not necessary to start a magazine, it is helpful for you to add in your profile image and a description of who you are. This allows others to get a sense of who you are. Click on the down-arrow next to where your username is located ("Signed in as greendtim" on Figure 5.11).

4. Click on the **CREATE MAGAZINE** button to begin the process to create a new *Flipboard* magazine. You

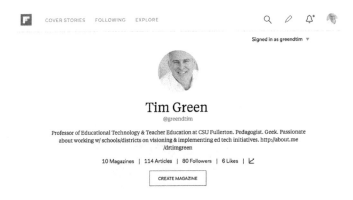

Figure 5.11 Screen shot of a *Flipboard* magazine. The image illustrates what the view would look like if you were logged in to your account and then clicked on your profile icon at the top right of the screen

will be asked to provide a title for the magazine, a description, and select if the magazine is public or private. Once you have created your magazine, it is ready to have resources flipped (added) to it.

Adding Resources to a Flipboard Magazine

There are two primary methods to add resources into your *Flipboard* magazine. One is to add an extension to your internet browser or to drag and drop a button to your internet browser bookmarks bar. You are able to add the extension or the button from *Flipboard*'s website by searching for "tools" before you are logged in to the *Flipboard* website. Flipping a resource using the bookmark button method is illustrated in Figure 5.12.

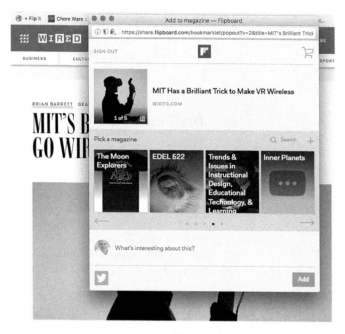

Figure 5.12 Example of adding a resource using the + Flip it bookmark button. This screenshot illustrates the menu that comes up when you click on the + Flip it bookmark button

The other method is to flip resources directly from the *Flipboard* website or app from *Flipboard* magazines that you follow. This is illustrated in Figure 5.13. When the cursor hovers over a resource, three icons appear. One of the icons is a red circle with a plus sign in it. Clicking on this icon will allow you to flip this resource into a *Flipboard* magazine you own or are a contributor. Only the owner of a *Flipboard* magazine can add contributors and make edits to a magazine.

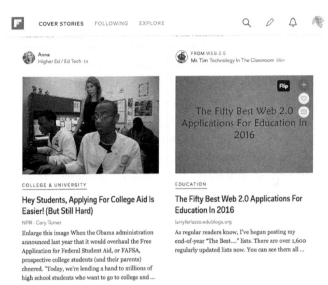

Figure 5.13 Flipping a resource into a *Flipboard* magazine. This figure illustrates what a screen looks like when the cursor is hovering over a resource that can be flipped into a *Flipboard* magazine you own or contribute

It is possible to add comments to the resources flipped into a magazine. Adding comments can be a way to further curate the resources you include. Take a look at Figure 5.12 where you can find *What's interesting about this?* Clicking on this area when you flip a resource allows you to add comments that show up below the resource that appears in your *Flipboard* magazine. This option will be available with either method (Figure 5.12 or Figure 5.13) you use to flip resources into your magazine.

Storify

Storify can be used as a web-based tool or as an iOs or Android app to create stories from various media found on the internet. Instagram, Flickr, Google, RSS feeds, Twitter, and YouTube are examples of where media can be gathered from to create a story. There are various formats that stories can take. A story can consist of only media, or it can be a combination of text that the story author has written along with media the author has gathered. You can locate story examples by searching using keywords in the Search Stories… area (see Figure 5.14).

Curating a Story Using Storify

Creating a story begins by clicking on the New Story button (see Figure 5.14). The story editor screen will appear after clicking on this button. The editor allows you to search for media from a variety of sources and then drag these on to the story—the blank white area on the left in Figure 5.15. Once you have media in this area, you can move them up or down to create how you want them to appear to your users. Clicking once in the blank area brings up a text box (see Figure 5.16) that allows you to add in your own text to create a story (or curate) the media you are including. In addition to adding in media and text, you can add a title to

Figure 5.14 Top menu when logged in to Storify. This figure illustrates various options available when logged in to a free Storify account

your story in the **Enter a headline** textbox along with a description of the story in the **Enter a description** textbox (see Figure 5.15). Once you have finished your story, click on the **Publish** button to make it available to others via a specific internet address that is created by Storify. There are other options available to your story—for example, it can be edited, embedded into a webpage, and shared via social media.

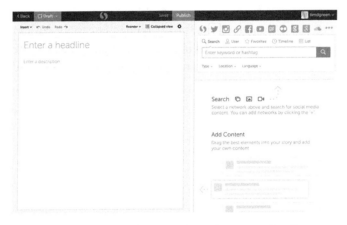

Figure 5.15 The Storify story editor. This screenshot illustrates the options you have when creating a story

Figure 5.16 Adding text to a story. This screenshot illustrates what appears when you click in the white area of a story

Summary

The primary goal of curating digital media is to help bring organization and meaning to a collection of information. There are three primary tasks to consider when curating digital media: *collecting* the digital media, *organizing* it in a meaningful way, and *sharing* it with others. We shared three tools—RSS, *Flipboard*, and Storify—that we regularly use to complete these tasks. While these tools work in different ways and result in distinctive final products, the tools still allow us to create OERs that consist of curated digital media.

6 | Copyright Considerations

As discussed in Chapter 1, open educational resource (OER) documents and media are freely accessible and open to use. Therefore, it may seem counterintuitive to discuss copyright issues when considering OERs. Despite the free and open nature of OER, copyright still applies. Whether you are adapting or using the work of others or designing your own OERs, issues of copyright should be carefully considered. In this chapter, we provide some fundamental ideas to consider regarding copyright when creating, modifying, and using OERs.

Copyright Essentials

According to Merriam-Webster, copyright is "the exclusive legal right to reproduce, publish, sell, or distribute the matter and form of something (as a literary, musical, or artistic work)" (Merriam-Webster, 2016). Copyright law, in essence, is meant to protect the copyright owner's ability to regulate how his or her work is used and to seek compensation for the work, if desired. While copyright law varies from country to country, there are basic principles that most countries follow. A few of these are as follows:

- Copyright is granted immediately upon the creation of a creative work in a tangible medium;

- Facts and ideas cannot be copyrighted;

- Only the copyright owner can reproduce or transmit publicly a work that has a copyright unless permission has been granted from the copyright owner or a fee (e.g., license or royalty) has been paid that provides for the work to be reproduced or publicly transmitted;

- There is a limitation as to how long a work remains in copyright; in the United States, for example, works that are published (i.e., made public on an unrestricted basis) after 1977 last for the life of the creator plus 70 years;

- Copyright owners can transfer copyright to another individual;

- Specific guidelines exist that outline the amount of a copyrighted work that may be used for educational purposes without obtaining permission from the owner (see Fair Use Guidelines);

- Works created by the U.S. government are not copyrightable.

The most comprehensive resource on U.S. copyright is the website maintained by the U.S. government at http://copyright.gov/.

The safest approach to using or modifying OERs is to obtain permission from the owner prior to using or modifying the document or media. If obtaining permission is not possible, there are limitations to keep in mind before using an OER for educational purposes as outlined in the Fair Use Guidelines for Educational Multimedia and Sections 107, 108, and 110 of the U.S. Copyright Act of 1976 and successive amendments including the Digital Millennium Copyright Act (1996). We outline some of the limitations from these guidelines and laws in Table 6.1.

While copyrighted media can be used for educational purposes, we caution about using it in OERs that are widely distributed unless you have permission from the copyright owner. The limitations described in Table 7.1 are for classroom use.

Fair Use Guidelines

Fair Use is a U.S. legal doctrine that "promotes freedom of expression by permitting the unlicensed use of copyright-protected works in certain circumstances" (United States Copyright Office, 2016b). The circumstances are those that use the work for a transformative purpose and for a limited time. A transformative purpose can include activities such as the following:

- commenting on the work,

- creating a parody of the work,

- criticizing the work,

- transforming the work into a derivative of the original.

Table 6.1 U.S Copyright Limitations of Media Use. This table illustrates various limitations of use for educational purposes of various copyrighted media assuming proper attribution is given.

Medium	Limitations	Use
Printed Material	• Articles, essays, or stories of less than 2,500 words; only 10% or 1,000 words, whichever is less, from larger works. • Poems less than 250 words; excerpt of 250 words from larger poems. • One cartoon, chart, diagram, image, or picture from a book or issue of a periodical. • Two pages from an illustrated work of less than 2,500 words.	• Students may integrate text into projects (e.g., multimedia). • Teachers may integrate text into multimedia for teaching purposes. • Teachers may make one copy per student from a legally owned copy; the copy is based on the limitations. • Workbooks or other consumables cannot be copied.
Audio	• Up to 10% of a musical composition (e.g., sheet music) can be reproduced, performed, and displayed.	• Students and teachers can use up to 30 s of a musical composition if used for educational purposes.

Images and Illustrations	• Up to 30 s of a musical composition can be used.	• Students and teachers can use illustrations, images, or photographs—following limitations—in multimedia used for educational purposes.
	• No more than five illustrations, images, or photographs can be used from a single artist, illustrator, or photographer.	
	• Not more than 15 illustrations, images, photographs, or 10%, whichever is less, from a collection may be used.	
Video	• 10% or 3 min—whichever is less—of motion video can be used.	• Students and teachers can use legitimately acquired video in multimedia projects created for educational purposes that does not exceed 10% or 3 min of a motion video.

Additionally, the fair use of a copyright work could include using it for research, scholarship, and teaching. There are four factors used to determine fair use of copyright material. These are (1) purpose of use for the copyright material, (2) nature of the copyrighted work, (3) amount of the copyrighted work used, (4) and the effects on the market value of the copyright material. The specific language of Fair Use and a detailed description of these factors can be found on the U.S. government's website by searching for Section 107 of the Copyright Law.

It is important to keep in mind that in the United States, the Fair Use Doctrine is actually a set of guidelines for court officials (judges) to apply when deciding whether a copyright violation has occurred. Educators use these guidelines to make their best guess at whether a judge would decide they have committed copyright infringement if a case were to go to trial.

Creative Commons

Within the open education resource community, there is a push for open licensing. Open licenses, according to UNESCO and the Commonwealth of Learning (2015), "seek to ensure that copying and sharing happen within a structure legal framework that is more flexible than the automatic all-rights-reserved status of copyright. They allow permissions to be given accurately, while releasing the restrictions of traditional copyright" (p. 2). Open licenses provide for content to be used without paying a license or access fee and without seeking permission. Open licensing allows for flexibility in the use and adaptation of documents and media for teaching and learning while still acknowledging the individuals who created the work (p. 2).

The Creative Commons (http://creativecommons.org/) has developed one approach to open licensing. Creative Commons licenses do not replace traditional copyright; rather, they build on it by providing a framework that allows creators to determine and communicate the rights they reserve (and waive) with work they have created. Creative Commons licensing provides increased freedom for others to use an individual's work without having to seek permission to use the work. As of the writing of this book, there are six Creative Commons licenses. The most restrictive is the Attribution-NonCommerical-NoDerivs that allows others to download and share the work as long as they give attribution, do not charge for the work, or use the work commercially. The least restrictive license is Attribution that allows for "others distribute, remix, tweak, and build upon your work, even commercially, as long as they credit you for the original creation" (Creative Commons, 2016a, para 10). Using a Creative Commons license for your OER provides others with a clear indication of how they can use, distribute, and build on the work you have created.

Attribution

Attribution, according to U.S. copyright law, is giving credit to the copyright holder of the OER when you use or modify the resource. When using OERs, a statement that includes the copyright year along with the copyright holder's name should be visibly included.

Providing correct attribution in educational media is important in terms of both providing accurate information and modeling ethical behavior. Attribution allows others to find the original item and its owner easily, and it maintains the tradition of "giving credit where credit is due." Bear in mind that proper attribution describes the work and its owner, not where you found the work. In producing digital media, some people incorrectly attribute works to search engines such as Google; proper attribution describes where the search engine found the item, not the search engine used to find it.

If you are modifying an OER, attribution is also important. It should be clear what aspect of the OER was used and modified. Proper attribution not only helps avoid confusion about the copyright owner, but it also helps you avoid any unnecessary violations of U.S. copyright laws.

Summary

It is important to note that copyright laws are complex. It is essential that you conduct your own investigation when you are concerned with whether you are in compliance with U.S. copyright laws when using OERs. The safest route to take with OER is to ask the copyright owner for permission to use or modify the work. We acknowledge that this is counterintuitive to the nature of OER, but we like to err on the side of caution. At the minimum, one should always give clear attribution to the author, creator, or producer of an OER when it is used or modified.

7 | Instructional Media Production and Evaluation

Once you decide to create open educational resources (OERs), you need to plan for production. Taking your idea from dream to reality requires some careful forethought. We agree with the statement attributed to Benjamin Franklin, "By failing to prepare, you are preparing to fail." Even the very best media production tools can only help with basic tasks; they cannot themselves design or create a quality product on their own. Effort is wasted without careful planning. Successful media production requires preparation, organization, and perspiration. By following good production practices, you will save time and energy, and you will wind up with an effective instructional media resource you are proud to share with students and colleagues.

Putting It All Together: The Production Process

Creating instructional media is a three-step process: preproduction, production, and postproduction. In preproduction, you come up with an idea and envision how that idea will look as a finished product. By "envisioning," we mean coming up with ideas, writing descriptions, creating sketches, or developing prototypes that help you define and articulate the finished product. This is the "dreaming-up" phase of the process, and experienced producers know this is something that requires a good deal of time and effort. A well-crafted and thorough presentation of your vision for the final product will help you through the second stage of the process (production) and ultimately save time and effort. After all, knowing where you are going is the first step to getting there.

Once you know where you are going with your media project and you have developed the scripts, sketches, or prototypes to help you envision the final result, it is time to begin the production step of the process. Production is when you begin to actually make the media piece itself. This starts with gathering all the resources you will need for the finished product. Most media producers use the notes, descriptions, and sketches created in preproduction to generate a list of everything necessary to complete the project. Once this list is complete, the next big step is gathering everything on that list and organizing the items into the product itself. Editing and revising are part of the production process. Once all the pieces are in place, you will need to review how well they work together and make adjustments to the overall presentation to make sure it achieves the desired result.

Postproduction is the third and final step in the process. This is the packaging and distribution phase. At this point, you are making the completed media piece available to others. You need to make sure that the work is accessible and usable to your intended audience. As an example, when we produce our biweekly podcast, it is in the postproduction phase that we upload a completed podcast episode to our blog and other media outlets, as well as announce the availability of the new episode through social media.

The Good-Cheap-Fast Production Triangle

The goal of most media producers is to create a high-quality product quickly and inexpensively. However, the recognized truth in practice is that you can only pick two of the following: fast, cheap, or good. You can create something really good quickly, but it will not be cheap. You can create something really good cheaply, but it will not be quick. You can create something really cheap quickly, but it will not be good.

The three steps, preproduction, production, and postproduction, have a bit of fluidity among them. Different media projects have their own requirements and best practices, and you will no doubt develop a production process that works best for you. Depending on the project, some aspects of preproduction might be considered production activities and some production activities might be completed during postproduction. In general, though, anything that consists of creating a vision for the finished product is considered preproduction, anything that involves actual creation of media is production, and anything that involves making the finished piece available to an audience is postproduction.

Keeping Track of Quality: Evaluating Your Work

Throughout the production process, it is important to continually evaluate your work. Checking and rechecking the project's quality help to create the best possible product. There are two types of product evaluation: formative and summative. Formative evaluation is the process of gauging the quality of the product while you are in the middle of the production process. This can take the form of getting feedback on your design notes or sketches from other educators or potential students, testing parts of a larger project, or getting feedback on drafts or prototypes of the entire product.

Summative evaluation is the process of gauging the quality of the product after the production process is complete. Most often, summative evaluation is conducted if you plan to revise the product or create new products based on the current product's design. Summative evaluation strategies include observation of the product in use and feedback from learners who use the product.

Choosing to conduct evaluations and the selection of evaluation strategies is up to you. However, we strongly recommend incorporating some form of evaluation into your production routine in order to answer the questions that include the following:

● Is this product doing what I want it to do?

● Is this product usable and useful for learners?

● Is this product an effective piece of instruction?

Is It Worth the Effort?

Another important evaluation consideration is whether the project itself is worth the resources and effort you put into it. In other words, is the potential return worth the initial investment? This is a question you should ask yourself about any project during the preproduction or brainstorming phase. As an example, years ago when Abbie taught eighth grade English and was learning to create computer-based media, he programmed a ten-question quiz on a reading assignment. Programming the quiz took hours of work; it would have been much easier and less time consuming to create the same quiz using pencil and paper. We certainly believe creating educational media is worthwhile, but we caution you to focus your own production efforts on things that are reusable and useful to the largest possible audience.

Sharing Your Work

Making your products freely available is what OERs are all about. Educators have a long and proud history of sharing their work with others to benefit learners. The OER movement is the most recent chapter in that history. Table 7.1 lists some of the most popular methods of sharing instructional media.

In addition to the popular sites for sharing resources described in Table 7.1, digital tools like *Flipboard* and YouTube can be used to create, find, and share OERs. We discuss both tools in previous chapters on digital video and digital media creation.

Table 7.1 Popular websites for sharing resources

Website	Web Address	Description
Creative Commons	creativecommons.org	Creative Commons allows individuals to share a wide variety of media and provides simple standard methods for permission and use.
MERLOT (Multimedia Educational Resource for Learning and Online Teaching)	merlot.org	MERLOT invites individuals to add to their collection of OER.
OER Commons	oercommons.org	OER Commons invites individuals to contribute work and provides creation tools to author lessons and modules.
TeacherTube	teachertube.com	TeacherTube allows individuals to create an account and share video resources. Similar to YouTube, TeacherTube has greater access in K-12 school settings.

Sharing on Social Media

Another excellent medium for finding and sharing OERs is social media. Social media tools such as Facebook, Instagram, and Twitter are currently popular among educators who use the tools to digitally connect with others to find ideas, have conversations, and share resources. We encourage you to explore social media tools to connect with others in order to share the OERs you create. If you are new to social media, it is important to consider the format of and the type of audiences that the various tools appeal to before embarking on using the tools. Each tool has a specific format that, in general, appeals to different demographics.

Final Thought

Always keep in mind that media constantly evolves. What you learn to produce today should help you produce new and different products tomorrow. When we began producing instructional media in the 1980s, we could not have guessed the development of media such as blogs or the distribution of media over the internet. However, the skills we developed producing "old" media helped us to master new media. Today's new media is tomorrow's "old," but the basics of production will no doubt apply just as they have since the first theatrical productions of ancient Greece.

We encourage you to develop both your skills with current new media, and your ability to see the larger picture in terms of what is trending and what is on the horizon. Learn how to use new media, and consider it as foundational knowledge for learning about tomorrow's media.

Summary

In this chapter, we described the production process and basic methods of product evaluation. We stressed the benefit of careful planning and the need to determine at the outset whether the project is worth the time and effort needed to complete it.

The production process itself is actually a three-step process of preproduction, production, and postproduction. Preproduction involves creating descriptions, rough sketches, and/or prototypes of the finished product in order to help you plan for the second step: production. During production itself, you gather all the pieces of the project and put them together to create the finished presentation. During postproduction, you make sure that your product is accessible to your intended audience. We also advised you of the fast-cheap-good production triangle: a good product can be created cheaply, but it will not be fast; fast and good, but it will not be cheap; or cheap and fast, but it will not be good.

In evaluating the quality of a product, there are two basic strategies: formative evaluation conducted during production, and summative evaluation conducted after the product is completed. These evaluation strategies are not mutually exclusive, and most designers use formative and summative evaluation strategies for each of their projects.

We provided a few resources for freely sharing the media you produce including Creative Commons and TeacherTube, which are particularly popular among educators. Freely shared educational media are considered OERs and follow a long tradition of educators sharing their instructional products with other educators.

References

Adobe Systems, Incorporated. (2016). About Adobe PDF. Retrieved from https://acrobat.adobe.com/us/en/why-adobe/about-adobe-pdf.html.

Allen, I.E. & Seaman, A. (2014). *Opening the curriculum: Open educational resources in U.S. higher education, 2014*. Babson Park, MA: Babson Survey Research Group.

American Printing History Association. (n.d.). History of printing timeline. Retrieved from https://printing history.org/timeline/.

Bergen, M. (2015). Google brings podcasting to Play Music, swinging at Apple's dominance. recode. Retrieved from http://recode.net/2015/10/27/google-brings-pod casting-to-play-music-swinging-at-apples-dominance/.

Brown, A. & Green, T.D. (2008). Video podcasting in perspective: The history, technology, aesthetics, and instructional uses of a new medium. *Journal of Educational Technology Systems, 36*(1), 3–17.

Brown, A. & Green, T. (Producers). (2016). Trends & issues in instructional design, educational technology, and learning sciences [Audio Podcast]. Retrieved from http://trendsandissues.com/.

Butterick, M. (2016). Butterick's practical typography. Retrieved from http://practicaltypography.com/point-size.html.

Ciccarelli, S. (n.d.). History of podcasting. *Voices.com*. Retrieved from www.voices.com/resources/articles/podcasting/history-of-podcasting.

Collier-Reed, B.I., Case, J.M., & Stott, A. (2013). The influence of podcasting on student learning: A case study across two courses. *European Journal of Engineering Education, 38*(3), 329–339.

Creative Commons. (2016a). Share your work. Retrieved from https://creativecommons.org/share-your-work/.

Creative Commons. (2016b). About the licenses. Retrieved from https://creativecommons.org/licenses/.

Domo. (2016). Data never sleeps 4.0. Retrieved from www.domo.com/blog/data-never-sleeps-4-0/.

Edison Research. (2015). The podcast consumer. Retrieved from www.edisonresearch.com/wp-content/uploads/2015/06/The-Podcast-Consumer-2015-Final.pdf.

EDUCAUSE. (2010). 7 things you should know about open educational resources. Retrieved from http://net.educause.edu/ir/library/pdf/eli7061.pdf.

Edutopia. (2014). Open Educational Resources (OER): Resource Roundup. Retrieved from www.edutopia.org/open-educational-resources-guide#graph3.

Elkeles, T., Phillips, P.P., & Phillips, J.J. (2015). ROI calculations for technology-based learning. *TD Magazine,*

January 2015. 42–47. Retrieved from www.td.org/ Publications/Magazines/TD/TD-Archive/2015/01/ ROI-Calculations.

Fernandez, V., Sallan, H., & Simo, P. (2015). Past, present, and future of podcasting in higher education. In M. Li & Y. Zhao (Eds.), *Exploring Learning and Teaching in Higher Education* (pp. 305–330). Berlin: Springer.

Gascoigne, B. (2001–present). History of writing. *History World*. Retrieved from www.historyworld.net/wrldhis/ PlainTextHistories.asp?groupid=3517&HistoryID= ab33&gtrack=pthc.

Haley, A. (n.d.). Type classifications. Retrieved from www.fonts.com/content/learning/fontology/level-1/ type-anatomy/type-classifications.

Heilesen, S. (2010). What is the academic efficacy of podcasting? *Computers & Education, 55*(3), 1063–1068.

Hew, K.F. (2009). Use of audio podcast in K-12 and higher education: A review of research topics and methodologies. *Educational Technology Research and Development, 57*(3), 333–357.

Kang, C. (2014). Podcasts are back – and making money. *The Washington Post.* Retrieved from www.washington post.com/business/technology/podcasts-are-back--and-making-money/2014/09/25/54abc628-39c9-11e4-9c9f-ebb47272e40e_story.html.

Manjoo, F. (2015). Podcasting blossoms, but in slow motion. *The New York Times*. Retrieved from www. nytimes.com/2015/06/18/technology/personaltech/ podcasting-blossoms-but-in-slow-motion.html?_r=2.

Merriam-Webster. (2016). Copyright. Retrieved from www.merriam-webster.com/dictionary/copyright.

Oxford Dictionaries. (n.d.). Podcast definition. Retrieved from www.oxforddictionaries.com/us/definition/american_english/podcast.

Parvizi, P. & Silverman, D. (2015). The future of podcasting. *Tech Crunch.* Retrieved from http://techcrunch.com/2015/07/18/the-future-of-podcasting/.

Rosenbaum, S. (2011). *Curation nation: How to win in a world where consumers are creators.* New York: The McGraw-Hill Companies.

Socha, B. & Eber-Schmid, B. (2014). Defining New Media Isn't Easy. *What Is New Media?* New York: New Media Institute. Retrieved from www.newmedia.org/what-is-new-media.html.

Tam, C. (2012).The effectiveness of educational podcasts for teaching music and visual arts in higher education. *Research in Learning Technology, 20,* 14919. doi:10.3402/rlt.v20i0.14919.

UNESCO. (2015). Open Educational Resources. *Communication and Information.* Retrieved from www.unesco.org/new/en/communication-and-information/access-to-knowledge/open-educational-resources/.

UNESCO and Commonwealth of Learning. (2015). *Guidelines for open educational resources (OER) in higher education.* Paris, France: United Nations Educational, Scientific and Cultural Organization and Commonwealth of Learning. Retrieved from http://unesdoc.unesco.org/images/0021/002136/213605E.pdf. United States Copyright Office. (2016b). More information on fair use. Retrieved from www.copyright.gov/fair-use/more-info.html.

William and Flora Hewlett Foundation. (2013). Open educational resources: Breaking the lockbox on education. Retrieved from www.hewlett.org/sites/default/files/OER%20White%20Paper%20Nov%2022%20 2013%20Final_0.pdf.

Index